DISCLAIMER

The UK Music Artist
A Practical Guide to Starting in Business

Stephen J. Pell ACCA CTA

PELLARTISTS

CONTENTS

ABOUT THE AUTHOR

Stephen Pell runs his own music entertainment practice, providing business management, international tax and accounting services to music artists, songwriters and producers. Formerly, he was a director in an international accounting practice where he specialised in international tax planning and the licensing of intellectual property for high profile individuals within the music and entertainment industries.

Stephen holds a Bachelor's degree with Honours from the University of Birmingham, is a Chartered Accountant and a Chartered Tax Advisor.

INTRODUCTION

"Work with the man when the man can help you make art…"

- Amanda Palmer

The music industry has been in turmoil over the last few years. It was almost brought to its knees by music piracy, poor business leaders and their reluctance to put the music consumer first.

Artists were signing complex contracts that alienated them and complex accounting practices became the industry 'norm'. Industry executives had the financial clout to hire the best accountants to cleverly conceal and reduce payments to artists in order to make up for the shortfall left by their drastically declining record sales.

What we are seeing now is an industry facing the future with new hope—more competent business leaders, more innovative and transparent business practices are being developed and new markets are opening up.

Don't get me wrong. There are still many things wrong with the music industry. The streaming model, for example, still needs to work itself out; artists are getting a raw deal, the larger labels are still squeezing artists to breaking point, and declining recording revenues mean that labels are less likely to take a gamble on unproven artists. But there is a new generation of music entrepreneurs leading the way

1

that provides genuine optimism. The question now isn't whether you have a future as a successful music artist in today's music industry, but more how can you take part in the new and emerging model in a way that you can take every opportunity that comes your way.

As an artist, you are not in a typical profession; careers can be very short-lived with earnings lumpy and precarious, so every penny counts irrespective of whether you're a DIY artist on the local gig circuit or an international superstar selling out stadium tours. A good business mind-set starts with ensuring you have an understanding that you are a business and that you will need the right people on your team to help you.

You are first and foremost an artist—your attention should of course be focused on developing your art. But as your career and earnings grow, it is very important that you understand that many people will have invested time and money in you and they will have done so because they believe in you and your earning potential, you will have made contractual commitments with some of these people (managers, record labels, publishers etc.). As an artist you will earn different types of income from many different sources and you ultimately face the same pressures as anyone else running a business, such as paying bills and making sure you have enough money to fund your lifestyle.

Moreover, your business operations will become increasingly international, meaning you will have to comply with not one set of tax laws but many. As an international artist things can get very complex very quickly and you need to make sure that you have a plan in place that is flexible enough to facilitate your successes and protect your earnings over the long-term.

Your art can have many chances of becoming successful—great songs are successful time and time again. As an artist you are the vehicle for these songs, and great artists make a song their own; but a great song has many owners, crosses genres, fashions and decades. And so, ensuring you set up your business in a way to best take advantage of the commercial opportunities that come your way over your career and beyond should be a priority.

There are a number of great books out there that will guide you through the complexities of the wider music business. This book will not help you get a record deal, tell you if your manager is ripping you off or explain the art of self-publishing. I have written this short book as an introduction to some of the issues and challenges you might face when starting out as a music artist and how to go about getting started with the setting up and administration of your music business. I will introduce you to some of the key advisors you'll need on your professional business team, what to look for when choosing them and how you'll know if they are doing a good job. I'll also talk you through some of the main business challenges you'll face at the start of your career and as it starts to take-off. Throughout this book I have tried to keep tax and accounting jargon to a minimum and illustrate the main points with examples. As well as helping you to understand the financial side of your music business, I will highlight some tax-saving opportunities as well as practical steps and dangers to bear in mind.

Over the years, I've seen artists who have benefited from the principals and ideas discussed in this book and others whose careers have suffered because they didn't understand or care for some of the key elements shared here. I have seen careers drastically cut short from poor business planning and I have inherited internationally-renowned artists who had been left with almost no money to live on. Starting a business entails a series of decisions which can seem overwhelming without the right players on your team. In order to succeed, you need to equip yourself with every tool at your disposal. As any coach will tell you, having a first rate attack (such as your manager or record label) won't guarantee a winning team without a first rate line of defence. Your professional advisor is your best line of defence and their expertise can help ensure the longevity of your career.

Knowledge is power—well, if not power, it certainly provides the foundation for informed decision making. Nobody will expect you to be an expert in business or accounting, but getting to grips with some of the discussions in this book will make you fairly unique among artists and may even provide you with a competitive advantage.

Understanding what lies ahead and when to take action could mean the difference between success and failure for some artists. The very fact that you are reading this book shows that you have the interest and desire to take action, which will hold you in good stead throughout your career.

This book should help give you an understanding of your music business and some practical guidance at various stages of your career, but ultimately, there is no secret to success in the music business. Like any business it requires smart planning, hard work and seamless execution.

How to use this book

I have written this book as an action book to provide a set of directions on how to navigate the complexities of your music business. Some parts will be relevant to you now, and other sections may provide a good point of reference at different stages of your career. Usually, the topics that grab your interest tend to be things currently happening in your life right now.

While you may not be a superstar artist yet, having an understanding of the challenges you will face as a superstar artist will put you in an excellent position as your music enterprise grows.

Part I looks at whether you have a business, the implications of ignoring the fact that you have a business and what you need to do to move things along.

Part II tackles some of the main business challenges you'll face as your career starts to take off.

Part III takes a look at the types of income and costs you are likely to come across as an artist or band.

Part IV talks about the importance of your professional business team, who makes up your professional business team, what roles they play and, importantly, when you need to hire them.

Part V explains how financial information can be used to your advantage, the administration you need to keep a handle on and what you should be asking your professional business team for.

Part VI answers some common questions asked by artists like you.

At the end of the book I have defined some key business terms that you may hear your business team talking about a lot. I have put these here as a point of reference in addition to adding more clarity and detail to some of the concepts discussed in the book. I have also included some examples of financial statements and reports you are likely to come across.

Throughout the book I have collectively referred to the professionals that help you run your business, tax accounting and administration as your 'professional business team.' This term does not refer to other professionals that help run your music business empire, such as managers, agents or lawyers.

This book is not a novel or textbook, so please circle or star passages you think you'll need, and fold over pages, stick paper clips on them or do whatever helps.

Finally, remember that tax planning and international accounting concepts are an extremely complex area and the relevant tax legislation, as well as government and international practices, can change quickly. This book is not intended to cover all the details required to advise properly on the issues highlighted. You should never take any action until you have spoken to a suitably qualified professional who can advise you based on your personal circumstances.

Let's get started.

PART 1: GETTING STARTED

Do I have a music business?

If it is your intention to make money from your music and it is no longer a hobby, then you have a business.

In short, if you are demonstrating your intention to make money with your music enterprise, such as entering into agreements with promoters, managers, publishers or record companies, and of course if you are already making money, you have a business. Your goal, as well as that of your business team, should be to generate as much money as possible by making your music profitable through selling records and filling venues.

I always enjoy talking to artists, in particular, getting to understand the concerns that they have. It seems to me that the biggest challenge, almost unanimously when starting out, is balancing band and work commitments. This is usually followed by the lack of cash in their pockets, particularly after making the decision to quit their jobs, so getting started as an artist is a testing time. Almost every artist I talk to says they absolutely "must" make money from their music but each of you will have difference reasons for this.

If this doesn't quite sound like you, and it is not your intention to make money from your music, then it is likely that you are doing it as a hobby. If you have a full time job and get together with friends a couple of times a month to play at your local pub in exchange for a few beers, then it would be difficult to justify that you are really in it for the money. From this point on in the book I will assume that you have decided to get serious about your music career and you are taking your first steps to superstardom.

Before I dive into this topic any further, please keep in mind the following:

1. You are a business
2. Your skills probably lie in your love of creating and performing
3. Your music career is not infinite
4. You should never underestimate the value of cutting costs

Let's talk about what I mean by the above.

1. You are a business

There is a common misconception among artists that you have to set up a company to run a business. This is not true—anyone can run a business, but there are many things to think about before you start that will need careful thought and expert navigation.

The reality is that, as an artist with commercial intentions, you are a business owner, and this should be taken seriously. You will encounter the same opportunities and threats as anyone else starting out in business and you will be treated the same as any other business owner by the government.

You are in the hot seat—you are the decision maker and ultimately, you are exposed to the risks and rewards associated with your enterprise. Of course your manager and record label may have something different to say about who burdens the risk (and therefore has higher stakes in the rewards), as they would argue they are making big investments of time and money in you. But the way I see it is that, while I agree there is risk in investing large amounts of money and time working with an unknown entity to raise your profile and getting you out there, they usually work with a number of artists which spreads out their risk considerably. On the other hand, you are working with them on an exclusive basis. Your music career is in their hands, and you may only have one shot at it. When you look at it from this perspective, I feel artists have more to lose by this arrangement—they usually sacrifice a lot to pursue a music career (you probably will have left another career before committing full time to music and the strain on your family and social life can be difficult). That said the financial and personal rewards can, of course, be enormous.

You should consider that you are capable of generating millions of pounds, you have the potential to make a big business out of yourself, and once this happens everyone will want a piece of you. Having a water tight, professional operation is a must no matter how much you go on to earn, but more so when the world is watching you.

2. Your skills probably lie in your love of creating and performing

In my experience, most artists get nervous or feel out of their depth when talking about the numbers in their business. I know that perhaps you wouldn't have gone into the music business if you wanted to be an accountant or tax advisor, and the corporate side to the music business may even make you feel uncomfortable. This is certainly not to say that you aren't good at it or that you are not able to fight your own corner and hold your own in the business world. There are many examples of financially and commercially astute artists who, over time, become confident with their business skills, setting up their own labels and managing their own artists. The music industry is full of commercial opportunities and entrepreneurs, and there are many savvy artists out there who take full advantage of their position, and I for one love seeing this.

But it's understandable if you don't start out as a savvy business person. After all, you are likely in the business of performing because of your love of creating and performing. While focusing on your passion for music is certainly the best place to start, it is also important to never forget that this is also your career and your livelihood. You need to make sure you are picking the right people to run your business operations. Once this is accomplished, you can then set your life on autopilot and focus on why you started down this path in the first place: to make music and entertain people.

3. *Your career in not infinite*

In most careers you can expect to have a professional shelf life of around 40 years, but this is very rarely the case as an entertainer in the music business. This means your concentrated earnings over a few years will need to be spread over a 40 year period and also provide enough for you to enjoy your retirement. Suddenly the money doesn't look so good.

You need to have the 'business mindset' even if you do not have the experience or expertise to run a business. By this, I mean you need to maximize every commercial opportunity to earn money, scrutinize your business expenses, and organize your business affairs to maximize your lifetime earnings. This means keeping tabs on the key members of your business team who help generate your income, such as your manager, and those members of your business team who safeguard your wealth, such as your accountant. Income from your music business will be lumpy, and preservation of wealth can diminish very quickly. You will need to have a realistic perspective on the lifespan of your career and plan accordingly.

4. *You should never underestimate the value of cutting costs*

You may expect me to chirp on about cost cutting, but let me explain the value in doing this:

For every £1 you earn, you have to pay your manager, agent, business manager and lawyer out of this (if they're on a percentage of what you earn). On the other hand, for every £1 you save, the whole amount goes into your pocket because you've already paid the costs of your manager, agent business manager and lawyer.

Let's look an example where your earnings are, say, £1,000,000. I have demonstrated in the table below how an additional £100,000 of income earned compares with saving an additional £100,000. For this example I will assume your management commission is 20%, your agent's commission is 10% and your business manager and lawyer each take 5%, for a total commission's payable of 40%.

	Example	Earn £100,000	Save £100,000
Income	1,000,000	1,100,000	1,000,000
Less Commission @ 40%	(400,000)	(440,000)	(400,000)
Sub total	600,000	660,000	600,000
Less Expenses	(400,000)	(400,000)	(300,000)
Net Profit	**£200,000**	**£260,000**	**£300,000**
Additional money in your pocket		£60,000	£100,000

By cutting your expenses, particularly your tax bill, you can put significantly more money in your pocket. This is just one of the many reasons why you should value the input of a good accountant.

When did my music business start?

Unfortunately, the answer to this question isn't black and white. It's a question of judgement.

As mentioned at the start of this chapter you'll first need to be sure that the music you are making is no longer a hobby. The reason for this is because the tax authorities want you to have a business status only when it benefits them first and foremost. What I mean by this is if they successfully argue that you do not have a business, and that it is in fact a hobby, then they won't allow you to claim any costs when you file your tax return. Ultimately this means you end up paying more tax.

Have in the back of your mind that as soon as you are in a position to present yourself to the world as a commercial artist, you will likely be able to begin benefiting from the tax benefits of having started a business. But of course remember that you need to pay tax on any profits you make too. In order to prove you are in business, the tax authorities will first look to see whether you have a profit-seeking motive.

In order to help evaluate whether you are making music with the intention of making a profit, compare your music business to a shop. For a shop, the business starts when you open the doors to customers. All the work beforehand is simply setting up your business. Once the doors are open, you are in business, even if you don't get any customers on the first day. A lawyer, for example, would be seen to have started their business when they start looking for customers, when they 'open the doors,' in other words. The same concept applies to artists. Your fans are your customers. Are you looking for them already?

Your first income streams are likely to be from live performances. Even though you're probably not making much money to start with, the tax authorities will consider that you have a profit seeking motive as a key indication you are in business, so keeping track of early income is very important in order to validate the existence of your music business.

The tax authorities are getting more clued into how artists are earning their money, and more importantly to them, how much they are earning. The UK tax authorities will also look at the number of shows you do each year to help them decide whether you are trading even if your earnings are minimal; the more shows you do, the more they can justify that you are trading. This is because another key indicator the tax authorities use to see whether you have a business is the frequency and number of transactions taking place. Regularly receiving money for playing gigs, even if you aren't receiving much money, can be an indicator to the tax authorities that you have a business.

The creative process is marked by fallow and fertile periods that are hard for the tax system to assess properly in the UK, and there has been considerable debate regarding changing the current rules as this does leave people early on in their careers at a disadvantage where they have long periods when they aren't earning money. For example, artists will usually only make social security contributions when they are making a profit over a certain threshold. If you have long periods when you are not profitable then you may lose out on important state benefits when you reach retirement.

You may be in the process of testing or developing your songs, or building your brand before you are ready to go to market with your creation. You may ask whether you still have a business even though you are not making any money at the moment, and the answer to this is yes if you meet the above criteria. On the plus side, if you are not earning any money, then you will not have any tax to pay, but remember you will still be required to file a tax return.

Usually you will start out in the business world as a sole trader. Some people assume that 'sole trader' means one person working on their own, but this isn't necessarily true. Being a sole trader actually means you take full personal responsibility for the running of the business – you can still hire staff if you wish to do so.

Being personally responsible for the business as an individual means you get to keep all your business's profits after you've paid income tax on them. However, because the law sees you and the business as essentially the same thing, you are personally responsible for any losses your business operations make. This may mean that your personal assets, such as your house or car, may be at risk if you don't pay your debts.

As a sole trader you must pay income tax on your profits, make national insurance contributions and complete a tax return every year.

There are a number of other ways to operate your business that helps to separate your business from your personal assets and that could reduce the amount of tax you pay each year. These include using limited companies and partnerships. I will explore these options and how to structure your business in more detail later on in the book.

But what if I earn very little from my music?

If you work for yourself you must register for Self-Assessment with HM Revenue & Customs within three months of becoming self-employed, or you could risk a £100 fine. There is no minimum age at which a person must pay income tax. What matters is your income—if it's below a certain level during a given tax year you won't have to hand anything over to the taxman. If it's higher, you will face a bill.

Income tax in the UK is a "progressive tax" – in other words, the rate rises with your income. Everyone has a personal allowance, which is tax free. You will only have to pay tax on the income you earn above this level. For most people (although there are exceptions) you can earn up to £10,600 in the 2015/16 year before you need to start paying tax.

For example, your band may have four members, and as a partnership you earn £50,000 in the 2015/16 tax year. You have costs of £10,000 to deduct against your band income and you split the profits equally between you, leaving you with £10,000 profit each for the year. Assuming you have no other income, no income tax will need to be paid by each band member as your individual profits are less than the £10,600 annual allowance.

In summary, you will need to carefully consider your circumstances. If you are unsure as to whether you have started a business always seek professional advice. Once it has been established that you have started to trade, you will need to register with the tax authorities so that they can keep track of you. This is something you can do yourself or, if you'd prefer to work with a professional right from the start, this is something your accountant can do for you.

What if I bury my head in the sand?

You can probably guess what is coming here…

If you do not tell the tax authorities you are trading, the situation could be serious. This is because you may be charged penalties for failing to report your income and there is a risk of prosecution.

You may think that your personal manager has all this in hand. In some cases they may be able to help, but ultimately the responsibility lies with you to make sure you communicate accurate information to the tax man. Tax and accounting rules can be complex, and personal managers may not be qualified to advise you on these matters.

A common misconception among artists starting out is who the 'tax man' really is. The tax man is not your accountant or business manager but rather a government body whose sole responsibility is to collect as much tax as possible from you. In the UK the 'tax man' is called HM Revenue & Customs, which is often abbreviated to 'HMRC'. Your accountant is the one on your side making sure you don't pay too much tax, keeping you on the right side of the law by accurately preparing and filing your tax returns and letting you know how much tax you need to pay and when you need to pay it. The other players on your professional business team and who are also on your side are your business manager and tax adviser. I will discuss their roles in Part IV.

What the tax man wants:

1. to collect tax on all your income
2. to ensure you are claiming only business costs

If the tax man finds out that you have not declared income on which tax is due, you may be charged interest and penalties on top of any tax bill, and in more serious cases there is even the risk of prosecution and imprisonment.

The tax man will actively search for non-registered businesses and un-declared or under-declared income. They get information on you from a variety of sources, such as online searches, door to door enquiries, reports from members of the public and investigations into other businesses.

If you think about it, information on you and music artists is, generally speaking, incredibly easy to obtain. Show dates and ticket prices are extremely easy to find with only a few minutes of online research, and a quick calculation based on ticket prices will let them know how much income you are earning. Press releases and media outlets will help them identify whether you have signed recording and publishing deals, the date you signed them, and ultimately, whether you have income that should be declared.

If you fall into the category of not taking action or you didn't know that you have to declare your income, don't panic! You will generally benefit from disclosing the position voluntarily to the tax authorities as soon as possible and co-operating fully before they suspect anything. If you do this, it's unlikely to lead to prosecution and should help reduce any penalties too. I recommend that you should speak to a qualified accountant or tax advisor should you want to report your situation to the tax authorities.

Ignoring that you have a business could mean that you miss out on a number of early planning opportunities that could save significant amounts of money for you—not just in the first year, but every year. For example, you could discuss with your accountant whether it would save you more money running your business as a company or partnership, whether you should register for VAT and even assessing the best structure to have if you are loss making. I will discuss these concepts in more detail later on in the chapter.

Another point to consider is that the results of any tax investigations will not likely surface until a number of years after you were required to report your taxes. As well as being an emotionally difficult and costly process, it could also be detrimental to your music career. If it became public knowledge that you have a history of evading your taxes, it could seriously harm your records sales and endorsement opportunities. The public doesn't like tax dodgers, and this is particularly prevalent at the moment with the likes of Apple, Google and Facebook in the headlines. These global corporate giants are diverting profits from countries, such as the US or UK where they would be highly taxed, to so called "tax haven" countries where there is little or no tax. What they are doing is actually legal and known as tax avoidance, as they are using legal loopholes and complex arrangements to circumvent income from being taxed in the US or UK—not paying your taxes or declaring income is an entirely different matter and called tax evasion. This is a criminal offense. Unfortunately, it can even get worse—record companies and managers may use this as leverage against you when it comes to renegotiating your deals or may even drop you altogether. A few reputations in the music industry have been recently tarnished from such tax scandals. I am pleased to say this has not happened to anyone I have worked with, but it certainly can and does happen.

If you have that 'guilty' feeling when reading this then I suggest you speak to an accountant. Don't worry—they won't tell you off if they're nice! Professional advisors, such as accountants, will help you become compliant with the rules and regulations as efficiently and cost effectively as possible. Getting into a good compliant mindset early on will put you on a great trajectory as your business grows and becomes more convoluted.

What do I need to do next?

Hire an accountant

So now that you've established you have a business there are some legal requirements out there that you need to make sure you navigate accurately and on time.

A good accountant will manage all the legal aspects of your taxes from registering you with the tax authorities, calculating how much tax to pay and when to pay it, as well as making sure all documents are filed on time on your behalf.

They will also help you decide which legal structure is right for your business before you register for taxes and start trading. It's important to understand the different risks and benefits before you choose—whether you set up as a sole trader, limited company or partnership. The way you structure your business will affect all of the following:

1. the amount of financial risk you're taking on
2. the way you'll need to pay tax and report to the tax man and other government bodies, and
3. how much control you have over how your business is run.

Large crowds, dancing, alcohol, drugs and a host of other elements are a breeding ground for injury and personal liability cases particularly for artists on the road. While insurance should cover these risks, ensuring that each venue or promoter has adequate cover is a difficult and time consuming job. And even where you have insurance cover, it may not cover cases of negligence, and the cover may not apply in all situations or all jurisdictions. This is why I would strongly recommend setting up your business with limited liability protection as a major objective to catch anything that might fall through the net of the insurance companies.

When you set up a limited company, you're creating an organization specifically to run your business. This separates your business dealings from your personal finances, and any profits belong to the company. The profits will be liable to corporation tax (2015 rates are 20%), but once this is paid the profits can be shared amongst the owners of the company.

A limited company will pay you in one of two ways or a combination of both: salary or dividends ('dividends' are what we call payments to the owners of a business—employees for example can't receive these types of payments unless they own a share in the company). Major tax savings can be achieved by carefully planning how these are paid out to you, but you will need an accounting professional to work this out for you based on your personal circumstances and income needed to fund your lifestyle. For those who are new to setting up a business, it can be very surprising to learn how much money can be saved in taxes by setting up your company and income structures in a way that best suits your specific situation.

An accountant can help you with the above and advise you on a suitable and robust structure for you based on your personal circumstances and goals. Unfortunately, there is never a 'one size fits all' approach but getting your trading status right with the help of an accountant is the first step towards launching your business. Accountants can also be retained as an 'agent' to deal with your tax affairs on your behalf. I will discuss what to look for in your professional business team in great detail later on in the book.

Make sure you have clear business processes in place

Some artists decide to keep a handle on their own business administration to start with to save on costs, but more often than not, this gets relegated to the bottom of their to-do-list. The main reason for this is that there are always seemingly more important things to be doing, like making and performing music that will earn them some money. It's hard to argue with these priorities but if you want to handle your business administration yourself to start with it's something that needs to be taken seriously. You will need to decide who in your band is responsible for collecting income and making payments (usually the most organized member) so make sure you delegate these responsibilities early on. Sometimes your manager may be able to keep business records for you, but make sure you find the extent of work that they will do for you.

To help you with your business processes, here are some common issues that I have seen a lot in practice and some tips on how to be better prepared.

1. Not doing any organization of paperwork until it's too late—this is probably the most common mistake. The work piles up–probably in a shoe box–and you get further and further behind to the point where you never have the time to catch up. The more you try to hide from the problem the more it will occupy your thoughts.

2. Not using software–there are many electronic bookkeeping systems that are easy to use for people with no bookkeeping experience. You could also use Microsoft Excel if you have a worksheet formatted in the right way to accurately record your business transactions.

3. Not having a separate bank account–if you mix your business and personal finances you're just making life more difficult, not least because you will have to separate it all out when it comes to tax return time. The first thing to do when you've set up your band is to acquire a bank account.

4. Not filing bank statements in order–it sounds simple, but you'd be amazed how many people don't do it. What happens? You give your statements to your accountant and they phone back telling you you're missing statements. This means you've just paid your accountant (who is probably quite expensive) to organize your bank statements, when you could have saved money by doing it yourself.

5. Not have a filing system for your costs–have two files, one for paid invoices and the other for unpaid invoices. When you pay an invoice, write the date and method of payment on the invoice. Once paid, move it to the paid file. Keep both files organized alphabetically.

6. Not paying by card or transfer–your bank will do most of your bookkeeping for you for free. How? If you pay by card, direct debit or electronic transfer, a permanent record of the transaction is provided on the bank statement, detailing the date, amount and recipients name. In bookkeeping terms, that's a great start. So try and pay with cash as infrequently as possible.

7. Not retaining receipts–if you don't, you risk failing to account for certain expenses, which means paying more tax than you need to. Even relatively modest expenses can mount up, so keep a close record of every penny your band spends. Remember to keep receipts for even the smallest costs, such as stamps, stationery, bus and train tickets and record the mileage of all your music-related business trips.

8. Not budgeting for tax–although you may not have any cash at the moment, your accounts may show that you made a profit last year, which means you will need to pay tax. Make sure

you budget for this as you go, so you won't get any great shocks at the end of the year. Open a deposit or business savings account and put money aside for your tax. Saving 25-30% of all income you receive likely means you'll easily be able to pay your tax bill.

When you start becoming successful your time will get eaten up by touring, writing and recording, and the number of transactions will significantly increase and become more complex—you will need to think about hiring a bookkeeper or accountant to help you out. If, on the other hand, you're happy keeping the work in house for now, I can help you along by providing you with a formatted excel workbook specifically tailored to artist's starting out complete with bookkeeping instructions and invoice templates. For your free copy please get in touch by emailing info@pellartists.com.

Get your insurance sorted

Every day your music business faces the risk of financial disaster from occurrences outside your control, whether it is theft or vandalism of your music equipment or someone gets injured at one of your shows. Getting your insurance right is the first line of defence if something goes wrong, and undoubtedly things will at some point.

If you employ someone in your music business, you are required by law to have employers' liability insurance which will cover you against claims made if they injure themselves. If you don't have employers' liability insurance you are liable for prosecution, even if an accident doesn't occur.

While not legal requirements, there are several other types of insurance that should not be overlooked for your music business:

- Cancellation and Non-Appearance Insurance
- Liability Insurance
- Travel Insurance
- Business Insurance
- Cash Insurance

- Directors' and Officers'
- Office Combined
- Equipment Insurance
- Errors and Omissions
- Recordings
- Business Interruption
- Confidential Life Cover
- Disability Insurance
- Property Building and Contents

There are specialist insurance providers that understand the issues and challenges facing new artists and have straight-forward policies that provide the cover you need at an affordable premium. Further, they will also understand the nuts and bolts required when performing internationally.

Accountants and business advisors with genuine music industry experience and expertise will be able to introduce you to reputable, specialist insurance brokers, as accountants and business managers cannot usually provide this advice to you.

In this chapter we've discussed whether or not you have a business and some of the important steps that you'll need to take to move your business in the right direction. Perhaps you will have established whether you need to take any action right now. But this is just the beginning. In the next chapter, get ready to dive into some real life business challenges faced as music careers start to take-off.

PART II: TEN BUSINESS CHALLENGES FACING ARTISTS

Over the years I have worked with artists at various stages of their careers, from those still searching for the right record deal all the way through to the international superstars of today. There are common issues for every artist when starting out, but also as their profiles start to grow internationally.

A lot, but not necessarily all, of the common challenges can be mitigated by having a good professional team, which is why I cannot stress the importance of this enough. Unfortunately, I have seen cases where artists have been poorly advised. It cannot be expected that artists will know all the issues they will face, but being guided by advisors who do not have an awareness of some of the main issues can be extremely detrimental to your career. After all, you are unlikely to get more than one shot at your music career, so it's best to get it right from the start!

The challenges you will face taking your first steps in the music industry will primarily be concerned with making enough money to support your music activities and living costs. Balancing band commitments with other working commitments can also be tricky, as well as getting labels and publishers to commit to you. However, things can move forward extremely quickly in this business, and it's best to be ready for a whole new set of challenges as your career and profile moves to the next level.

I have pulled together my list of ten common challenges facing more established artists in today's climate. I have intended this section to highlight some of the key areas that need expert attention. As I'm coming from the point of view of a business advisor, your wider business team may have a different list of priorities. Typically, the key issues I consider important (in no particular order) are:

1. Getting the business structure right
2. Ensuring limited liability protection
3. Managing withholding taxes effectively
4. Reducing double taxation
5. Regular access to useful financial information
6. Ensuring compliance in overseas countries like the US
7. Managing international insurance
8. Making sure you have enough cash
9. Planning for social elevation and future financial security
10. Protecting your name and artistic creations

1. Getting the business structure right

As your profile and earnings grow, it is vital that you have the right business structure in place. The right structure for you will depend on a number of factors, including the need for limited liability protection (as discussed in Part I), and for efficient tax treatment of your global earnings. It's also important to compare the legal and tax benefits of any structure with the costs of setting up your operations and the costs you have to pay every year to run them.

When planning your structure correctly, your advisor will take into consideration your current and projected income levels, where you are working and living as well as your lifestyle and investment needs. This will include looking into the future as far as possible to spot any opportunities and threats you could face by structuring your business in a certain way. Let's now look at an example of what could happen if you fail to take account of your long term goals, which include moving to the US to elevate your career.

Imagine you write an album that you self-publish and you sell on the internet. Because you live in the UK your accountant tells you about the advantages of a UK limited company. Therefore you transfer your rights in the album to a new limited company at start-up and trade via the company.

Five years later, the company becomes profitable and generates royalties of £100,000 each year. You decide to relocate your company to the US as you discover a commercial opportunity there. In fact, there is a problem with you personally moving as the rights in your music are locked into the UK company. Any transfer of the rights out of the UK company would result in a tax charge to the UK company, based on the market value of those rights, which is likely to be substantial if they're generating £100,000 each year and the original cost was minimal.

Therefore, the fact that you never set foot in the UK after you leave would not stop the UK tax man from taking 20% of the profits of the company. If you decide to move abroad the other disadvantage of having a UK company is that you can't completely sever your ties with the UK. If you're trading as a sole trader you won't have any of these problems as you can just carry on your music business overseas without any further UK tax charges, which is why the way you set up your business initially is so important and dependent on your long term musical goals.

Importantly, whether you are a solo artist or in a band will determine the kind of structure you should have in place. For example, a partnership structure may be more appropriate for a band with multiple members rather than a UK company. This is particularly the case when band agreements are contentious and/or have complex profit split arrangements.

Not many people know this, but as soon as you start working together as a band, you've already formed a partnership. Any group of people working towards a common goal with the aim of making a profit are recognised under UK law as forming a partnership—this has major implications if things go wrong down the line. From a legal point of view, if no partnership agreements are drawn up you and your band members will have an equal share in the assets of the band (i.e. what the band owns like equipment bought with the bands money and the name of the band) and also any profits earned by the band. If the band splits up, then all of the assets and income will need to be divided up equally, and this could get messy if you don't have an agreement in place as to who has what. For example, how can you split a band name four ways?

Legally speaking, even if only one member leaves the band, the partnership is deemed to have ended. In addition, the band member who left could stop you and your other band members using the band name. That's what happened to Pink Floyd when keyboard player Roger Walters left—he decided to keep the name and in the legal battle that followed the lawyers were the only winners.

Just to demonstrate how important this concept is, not only does the partnership share in the profits and assets of the band, but also everyone has an equal share in the liabilities. This means that even if the band somehow gets into debt, you'd all shoulder the debt equally—it doesn't matter who in the band incurred the debt. If something really terrible happened like your lead guitarist stage-dives and injures (or even kills a fan) at a show, you're all equally responsible in the eyes of the law.

The good news is that there are ways of structuring your business affairs that help protect you and your band members, in particular through limited liability entities which I will discuss next. But do not underestimate the importance of ensuring legally binding band agreements are drawn up as early as possible as you never know when bubbling issues could surface.

As global and domestic rules and regulations change so will the suitability of your business structure. For example, the tax treatment of earnings in the UK often change each year and can change drastically depending on the political party in power. The new tax rules may negatively affect your existing planning and there may be a better alternative to your existing business structure.

Typically, your tax advisor or accountant will evaluate all your business activities and come up with a solution that meets your goals. Often, superstar artists end up with a complex web of entities to achieve this sort of resolution which can be expensive and time consuming to run but inevitably lead to significant tax savings and wealth preservation.

2. Ensuring limited liability protection

Artists often enter into contracts and receive income in their own names, particularly at the start of their careers. We saw how in Part I operating as a sole trader tends to be the starting position where no planning is implemented and in this chapter how partnerships are deemed to form the default position of a band.

While this is straightforward, it can leave you and your band members personally exposed to issues like the safety of fans at shows, or equipment failures. This is particularly acute in countries like the US, which has a more litigious culture. A UK limited company, for example, would provide another layer of legal protection in case of litigation.

Recently a fan sustained significant spine injuries after he was trampled to the ground at a metal concert and he claimed negligence on the part of the promoter. The promoter was accused of failing to provide adequate security for its customers. The band were not named in this particular lawsuit but could have quite easily been sued, and in turn sued by the promoter. They were seeking $75,000 in damages. As the band entered into the contract for the performance using a separate legal entity (i.e. a company), the lawsuit will have been with the contracting legal entity and not with the band members individually, meaning they cannot go after their personal assets—only the assets held in the company would be at risk.

Having a separate legal entity to furnish your services will not provide protection against every eventuality like manslaughter, for example, where you would be held personally responsible, but it will provide you with much more protection as well as helping to indemnify other band members from individual acts that misrepresent the band. As it happens, the front man of the same band was involved in another altercation a few years earlier and was arrested in the Czech Republic on suspicion of manslaughter, after a fan died stagediving at one of their concerts. The front man was later acquitted of all charges but it goes to show how things can go wrong.

Limited liability is not restricted to companies but can also apply to certain partnerships, which can also be advantageous for tax purposes.

3. Managing withholding taxes efficiently

As you start to earn income from touring in multiple countries you will increasingly have to deal with the local tax authorities in those countries, who hold back tax from the income paid to you. These are known as withholding taxes. Withholding tax rates vary considerably by country, but can be as high as 40% of your income in some countries. The US, for example, levies federal tax at 30% and an additional tax of 7% or more in some US states.

Without getting too technical, you can reclaim some of the tax back so long as you receive the relevant withholding tax certificates from the respective tax authorities. Alternatively, under some circumstances they can be treated as business costs. Think of these withholding tax certificates as money. Make sure you have someone collecting them for you as you'll need them when you file your tax returns in order to claim the valuable tax credit.

You will only be able to see the cash benefit of using these withholding tax certificates when it comes to paying your tax in the UK. As I'm sure you will agree, this is not an ideal position for you to be in as an artist as you'd rather have the cash in your pocket upfront, rather than getting some of it back many months later. And of course you may not even be in a tax paying position to benefit most from the withholding tax certificates. You may have expensive production and recording costs to pay, and if not managed correctly, it can lead to very real cash flow problems for everyone who wants to get paid. If, say, 30% tax is withheld at source, you still have to pay other commissions of, say, 40%. Effectively, you have 30% of that show fee to pay your touring expenses and to split amongst your band—cash flow will be tight, I promise you!

Traditionally promoters have split show fees between production costs and the artist performance fee to lower withholding tax. But artist's performance income has come under increasing scrutiny by tax authorities in developed countries over the last few years, and the opportunity to avoid foreign taxes on this type of income is getting harder to legally accomplish. However, many accountants and tax advisors that understand the music business have a number of tricks up their sleeve to help reduce the tax held back by other countries.

4. *Reducing double taxation*

An often overlooked issue facing many touring artists today is the problem of double taxation. Essentially, we accountants like to look at the overall rate of taxation you pay, rather than simply looking at the corporate and personal tax rates in isolation.

The term 'double taxation' refers to being exposed to tax more than once on the same income. I fear that probing much further into this concept will result in glazed eyes, but take a moment to consider the following:

Say you earn £5,000 for a live performance and this gets paid to your UK company. This income will be taxed at the company rate first (at around 20%), and when you take the money out of your company you will be taxed again at income tax rates. If you are registered for VAT you will need to charge VAT on this income too (often around 20%), which is a further example of double taxation.

Say you earn $5,000 for a live performance in the US. They will tax this income at say 30% before this is paid to your personal company in the UK. This income will still be taxed at corporate rates in the UK on the total fee (i.e. $5,000) and again at income tax rates when you take the money out of your company.

There are number of strategies in addressing the issues of double taxation, which range from ensuring you have a business structure for international business and the appropriate business entities as well as correctly applying international law and tax treaties. Alternatively, there are situations when it makes sense to file a tax return in a foreign country which has withheld tax. You will need an advisor with global expertise to get this right, country by country, and proper tax planning needs to be a strategic part of planning any international touring.

5. Regular access to useful financial information

I will discuss in detail the benefits of financial reports later on in the book, but having regular reports that you can actually use to make decisions is critical if you want to succeed.

Running an international tour is extremely complex, and financial reporting and record keeping can be particularly demanding. As your profile grows, the scale and complexity of tour activity will also grow.

Even at an early stage in your career, huge value can be added through up-to-date reports which track costs against budgets and best practice touring benchmarks. What I mean by this is that an accountant or business manager with experience in reporting on artists tours will be able to compare your results against those of other artists, identifying where you are over spending so that you can address any problems early on. I will go into more detail with the types of reporting that are useful in Part V.

An expert advisor who can work closely with your team will make your touring business run much more smoothly and can generate major savings for you. Typically, a good tour accountant will handle the following for you:

- Withholding tax mitigation and planning
- Multi-currency treasury management
- Production reports and reconciliation
- Benchmarking analysis

- Budget reviews and variance analysis
- Processing of purchase invoices and payments
- Withholding tax certificate collection, correspondence and follow up
- Foreign social security compliance
- Application for certificate of residence
- Review and renewal of insurance policies specifically for worldwide touring

Having access to up-to-date financial information will enable you to make business and life decisions, such as when you can afford to buy a house, employing a new band member, buying some expensive equipment and very importantly, how much you can pay yourself while keeping your touring commitments afloat.

I have seen bands in the past leave their tour accounting and financial performance appraisals to their management team. While managers ultimately like to make sure they have their finger on the pulse of your business and earnings, they too are best focusing on the commercial and operational aspects of your business and career, and details can be left in the cracks when not overseen by those experienced at dealing with these specific situations.

6. *Ensuring compliance in overseas countries like the US*

As your career develops, you will find yourself spending more and more time in your key markets, like the US. I have used the US as an example here as it's very much seen as the Holy Grail to crack 'America', but the same applies for any country you spend a large proportion of your time in. When you start spending lots of time in other countries, things can get very complicated with your tax position. You may hear people talking about their 'residence status' and that they have a 'set' number of days that they can stay in a country before the tax man gets them. This is something to watch out for and to get expert advice on as it is not as straight forward as you think. These days, it is not enough to spend over half a year in a low tax country to avoid tax.

Many advisors in the US, unsurprisingly, hold a US-centric perspective, and struggle to provide the right advice for clients outside the US. On the other hand, there often comes a point when registering for tax in the US makes sense for people who tour in the US but do not live there. You will need expert advice on this issue, as well as help with the practicalities, and are best served by advisors with genuine global expertise.

When you have earned certain types of US source income, or when you have spent over half the year in the US, you may be required to file a US tax return. Additionally, when you spend more than 120 days in the US in any 12 month period, certain other forms must be filed. The penalty at the time of writing is $10,000 per return if you do not file these returns, so take note and ask a professional advisor if you're not sure!

There are a range of administrative issues which non-US artists face when touring in the US. Not least is the visa application, which needs to be scheduled well in advance, and for which experience presenting the required information in the right way is key to speedy approval. Equally, obtaining a social security number is much quicker and easier when done by an expert advisor.

7. *Managing international insurance*

I discussed insurance generally in a previous chapter, and here I will reiterate that having the correct insurance in place is critical for any touring artist. Do not think that you do not need insurance because you operate through a limited company. Insurance is there to protect a whole host of other stakeholders too, and there are always instances when directors of a limited company can be held personally responsible.

Accountants are generally not qualified or regulated to advise on insurance or investment matters. Instead you will need to speak with a specialist insurance adviser or insurance broker. In my experience, general insurance brokers tend to lack expertise in the live music industry. Paying the right amount in premiums and getting the right cover takes specialist expertise, just as choosing an accountant or lawyer with appropriate expertise is extremely important.

In addition it is well worth engaging the right advisors to ensure cross-border coverage is appropriate, and that international 'must haves' are in place at the right time.

8. *Making sure you have enough cash*

Cash is king when it comes to the financial management and of growing your business. The lag between paying commissions and tour costs and the time it takes to collect your touring income and royalties can be a problem. At its simplest, cash flow management means delaying outlays of cash as long as possible while encouraging anyone who owes you money to pay it as rapidly as possible.

An accurate cash flow projection can alert you to trouble well before it strikes but predicting the future is never straightforward. All we can do as accountants is make educated guesses that balance factors such as customer payment histories and our understanding of the types of costs and commitments you are likely to incur as a music artist.

Sooner or later, you will foresee or find yourself in a situation when you lack the cash to pay your bills whether these are business or personal. This doesn't mean you're a failure as an artist—this is very normal as no one can perfectly predict the future.

The key to managing cash shortfalls is to become aware of the problem as early and accurately as possible so that you can take action to address the perceived problem. To give you the best chance, an experienced music industry accountant can add tremendous value to this process.

9. *Planning for social elevation and financial security*

Tax and business planning, no matter how sophisticated, must be the foundation of your spending habits and desire for social elevation—

whether that's a new house, a new car, or even, a new private jet—although these really are reserved for the superstars!

A certain portion of income will always be required for personal expenditures, such as living costs. Your accountant will be able to help you with your personal cash flow and income needs, as well as telling you how much money you need to put away each month to buy that dream house.

Your accountant will also be vital when it comes to buying a property or taking out a loan, as they will be able to present and package your financial information to the bank in a way that the bank understands—and ultimately helps you to secure that loan.

Getting to a point where you have financial security isn't usually something that happens overnight. Achieving it takes a disciplined and balanced approach. To reach your financial goals you need to understand where you are, where you want to be in the future and what it'll take to get there. Only then can you establish a habit of savings to help you achieve your goals.

A starting point is tracking your monthly expenses and developing a list of things that you own, amounts that you owe and income. Once you've got your current 'financial house' in order, you can turn your attention to your future.

Everyone has hopes, dreams, goals and ambitions. Do you have a clear vision of what you want from your career and life? You've got to be specific about your goals–possibly more specific than you have ever been–because until you know what your ideal life looks like, you cannot come up with a plan to build it. Share your vision with your professional advisor and they can help you develop a plan to achieve it. Your professional advisor works for you, and providing them with a roadmap to where you want to go is the best way to ensure that you will receive guidance in that direction.

Accountants and other financial advisors have access to sophisticated tools that can help you see, in remarkable detail, where you stand, what you'll need to live your life comfortably and what it will take to get there. From this comprehensive viewpoint, you'll become well equipped to take control of your financial security and build a plan to live a financially comfortable life.

10. Protecting your name and artistic creations

Achieving financial security means more than accumulating wealth. It also means protecting your ability to create wealth. As a creator of art, you need to ensure everything you create is protected by law. It is essential that you protect your reputation and discourage people from ripping off your creations.

As an artist, you are always going to be a brand, as you hope that your name will be something that people recognize. The more successful that you are, the more likely is it that your band name, likeness and image will be recognized by members of the public, and companies will soon be knocking at your door wanting to put you on their products and associate themselves with your 'cool' artist brand and musical sound.

An important point to take on board is that you are a creator of intellectual property and your band name is a great example of this. Band names can be protected by trademarks. Registered trademarks are arguably one of the most valuable assets available to creators of intellectual property. Registered trademarks function to protect your reputation, establish quality, evidence exclusive ownership, discourage imposters, strengthen licensing and endorsement abilities and provide for significant damages in successful infringement actions.

Without registered trademark protection, extraordinarily valuable rights are subject to forfeiture, and in fact, others could make a filing in a desired class and then possibly prohibit or even make claims of infringement against you if you have no registered trademarks. Finally, the costs of filing for registered trademark protection are significantly less than dealing with infringement actions.

Your creations and art is protected in a number of other ways, primarily through copyright law in the UK. Your lawyer will be best placed to ensure you are fully protected.

It's important to be aware that copyright law is not the same in every country, although many principles can be similar. In the UK, as in the US, a copyright is secured when something is fixed in tangible form (something you can touch like music and lyrics written down). Unlike in the US, however, there is no registration procedure in the UK for copyrights. Essentially, a copyright exists when something is tangibly created, but you will need to be able to prove that you did indeed create it.

Copyright infringement applies to music, images, films or books and occurs when someone uses the whole or a substantial part of your work without your written permission. The same can apply if you use someone else's work without their permission. In the music industry this is particularly prevalent where samples of other people's songs are used. Therefore it is incredibly important your business team secures the correct clearances and licenses for using them. If it is found that there is a copyright infringement, then the matter is either resolved by mediation (i.e. coming to an out-of-court settlement) or by going to court. If you do go to court, the courts can stop the person from making further infringing use of the material, award the owner of the copyrights damages and make the infringing party give up the goods to the copyright owner. Deliberate infringement may also be a criminal offence, and the legal process of defending your copyrights can be incredibly expensive and emotionally draining. Therefore it is recommended that you discuss with your legal team any concerns you may have as early as possible so that they can ensure protection of these valuable assets and put your mind at ease so that you can focus and creating new income-generating copyrights.

I have talked you through some of the key challenges facing you as your career starts to take off. In the next chapter I'll guide you through the types of income you can expect to receive as an artist and of course where you'll need to spend some money.

PART III: TYPICAL ARTIST INCOME AND EXPENDITURE

In this chapter I will discuss the various ways artists earn their money and discuss the different income streams you should be aware of as an artist so that you can make sure you are collecting in every penny you are owed. A recent study showed that just 1% of artists earned 77% of all recorded music income in 2013. The music industry is a 'superstar economy,' so keep that in mind and have a realistic expectation of your earnings, particularly in the early days.

You will probably already have a sense of some of the different ways you can make money. Some forms of income are simple to understand, like the money you receive for playing shows. But music artists earn income form more sources than you might think, and this income can be generated from such things as your compositions, sound recordings, brand or knowledge of your craft. The income you earn will be divided into two separate types: performance income and royalties. The distinction between the two is mainly important for tax purposes and long term financial planning.

Performance Income

Let's start first with the income you earn from playing a show, as this is the most straightforward. Generally the money you generate here will be the result of negotiations between your manager or booking agent and the promoter of a venue. Both booking agents and your manager will get a cut of your show fee. Your booking agent, for example, will usually get a percentage of your gross fee and can often include the appearance fee and any benefits they negotiate on your behalf. For example, the payment you get for a particular contract could be a £5,000 appearance fee plus hotel and accommodation costs. The agent will usually want to add the value of the hotel and accommodation to the gross income in working out their fee. Sometimes your agent might negotiate additional non-monetary benefits and its here where a good accountant will be able to calculate an accurate value placed on such items.

If you are an established artist you may be able to get what's called a 'Guaranteed Minimum' included in the performance contract. This guarantees you will be paid a certain amount irrespective of whether the promoter sells enough tickets, therefore passing the risk to the promoter. Over and above the Guaranteed Minimum they may give you a fixed percentage of the promoter's net receipts. The contract should set out when any Guaranteed Minimum payment is to be made which is usually 50% up-front and the rest on the night of the performance

If you perform a show in a country that you do not live in, the promoter of the show is often required to hold back tax on this fee and pay you the balance. This is called withholding tax – we discussed this concept in Part II. Your accountant should advise you whether there are any advantages to structuring your touring services in a certain way, particularly when performing a run of shows overseas, where it may be appropriate to set up an overseas company. The promoter should be obliged to do all the necessary paper work to ensure they are correctly applying the tax law of their country and they should supply you with any forms you may need to complete to show the country in which you or your service company is based. However, some of these forms are not straightforward and you will need a suitably qualified professional to complete them on your behalf.

Your record label usually recognizes that your show fees will be minimal when you first start out as an artist and acknowledges you won't be profitable until your profile grows. It's difficult to make much money touring until you're a major star. Touring can be expensive, particularly when there are more than two people on the road. Record companies want you to break into markets around the world and will often commit to the payment of your costs on the road, such as promotional materials, travel and accommodation costs, purchasing or renting equipment and concert fees when you are self-promoting. Before a tour you will usually need to agree on a budget with them before they provide you with some income to pay for these costs.

Tour support is usually 100% recoupable from royalties from record sales but, depending on your bargaining power could be negotiated. For example, if you toured in Australia you could agree with your record label that the tour support is only recouped from your Australian record sales.

At the end of a tour or run of shows, it is usual to prepare a financial report showing whether or not you made a profit or loss. These reports help management and your record label determine whether or not the tour was a success. For management, the reports are important because they are the basis on which to calculate their fees. As an artist, you will find these important because they will show how much money your band earned on the tour.

One of my early experiences as an accountant was helping to resolve the problem of a band who had never formalized their agreement. One of the band members was also part of another band that had just signed a major record deal and was starting to become more successful than his original band. He naturally started having more commitments with his new band, and the first band had to hire session musicians to fill in for him from time to time. The situation became contentious when the band member (who was substituted for at certain live gigs) argued that he was still entitled to his share of the income from the shows he didn't perform at, as he 'was the band' and had made a big contribution to the songs. He argued that, without his input, the band wouldn't have been elevated to the position to play such shows. Needless to say, his other band members didn't agree with him, and it has taken many years and enormous legal costs to resolve the dispute. So pay attention and take care of band agreements and profit share agreements now. All of this could have been avoided with just a couple of hours planning.

Royalties

Overall, however, touring is fairly straightforward in contrast to the other aspects of income generated from the music business, so let's discuss the more complicated type of income you will earn from your music.

The first point to take on board is that every song has two copyrights which determine who receives what monies when a song is used to make money, and when you have a copyright, the income that this generates is called a royalty. In its simplest form, the two copyrights in your music are:

1. the musical composition, which includes the music and the lyrics
2. the sound recording, which is the performance of the music composition

Throughout this book I have referred to artists as those people who have signed to a record label, but of course artists can also be writers or performers of other people's music. The distinction is important because, depending on whether you are a writer, artist or performer, you will have different copyrights to the music and get paid royalties at a different rate. If you write, record and perform your own music then you get all the royalties, as discussed below.

As an artist you will receive royalties from five main sources:

1. Your record label
2. Your publisher
3. Performing Rights Societies
4. Advances
5. Other income

1. *Your record label*

When you sign to your record label you are usually agreeing to give the copyright in the recordings of the songs you make to them and in turn they will pay you a royalty from the money they make from selling and licensing your music. You will then split these royalties between the members of your band in accordance with what you agreed between yourselves (as I will discuss in the next chapter, it is helpful to set forth this agreement with the help of your professional team).

In reality, recording contracts are extremely complex and are a hotbed of debate in the music world. It is normal for record labels to pay your royalties twice a year, usually in March and September, but there are a number of other details to your recording contract that would be invaluable to receive advice on prior to signing.

2. *Your publisher*

When you sign with a publisher you are agreeing to give them rights to the musical composition, which includes the music and lyrics that you or the band wrote together. Note: these rights only include the words and the music composition, and not the beats, arrangement, or sound recording of the song.

Your publisher will work with you to develop your songs and your profile, including suggesting collaborations with other artists. They will collect income from your record label (known as a mechanical royalty) and from Performing Rights Societies and pay you a royalty based on a percentage of income they earn.

3. *Performing Rights Societies*

Performing Rights Societies are non-profit bodies set up to collect and pay to record companies, publishers and artists income collected from public venues where your music is played, such as pubs, clubs, bars, shops, exhibitions, or when your music is played on TV, radio and the internet. In the UK, there are two societies that do this job: PRS and PPL.

PRS is responsible for collecting money and paying royalties to the person who owns the music and lyrics of a song (the musical composition). If you have a publisher, these will be split between you and them, i.e. PRS will pay 50% of the money they collect on your behalf to you directly and the other 50% to your publisher.

PPL is responsible for collecting and paying royalties to the person who owns the sound recording (i.e. you record label) and to the artists who perform on the song. For example, if you have four band members and two members are not involved in writing the song, then those members would still get a royalty for their contribution to the sound recording despite not getting any publishing royalties. You may often hear these kinds of copyrights being referred to as 'neighbouring rights' or 'digital performance rights' in the US.

Not all countries have the same rules as the UK. For example, the US doesn't recognize these rights in the same way the UK does. This is a hotly debated area in music law at the moment and it is very conceivable that these royalty structures may change over time.

4. *Advances*

Typically, your record or publishing company will pay you an advance when you sign with them. This must be paid back to them out of the royalties you earn. This is called 'recoupment,' and it's rather like them giving you a loan. Sometimes this loan is not repayable to them if you do not make any money but you will need to check the wording of your contract very carefully to ensure that you will not owe funds if your royalties do not surpass the amount of your advance.

In addition to paying back their advance, artists often have to pay back many other expenses. These recoupable expenses usually include recording costs, promotional and marketing costs, tour costs, music video production costs, as well as other expenses. The record company or publisher is making the upfront investment and taking the risk (or so they say), but you will eventually end up paying most of the costs. While all of this can be negotiated up front, it tends to be the norm that you pay most of these expenses out of your royalties.

5. Other income

Licensing your music for use in films, television shows, advertisements and video games can be very lucrative. These are usually negotiated and arranged by your record label and publisher and are called "sync" licenses.

You can earn income from other intellectual property rights that you own, such as your band name, image and likeness. For example, you can sell merchandise with your logo on it or license these rights to companies that can make and sell these for you. The income you earn from this will usually be in the form of a royalty. The same applies if you endorse a company's products or if they want to associate themselves with your band in anyway. It is extremely important that you protect these rights, as they can become extraordinarily valuable as your profile builds.

As a successful artist you may well earn additional income from investments, such as purchasing property where you may receive rental income or income from shares where you may receive dividends.

It takes money to make money

So we've looked at where your income will come from. It's an old but true saying that it takes money to make money, so let's run through some areas where you will probably need to spend some money in your music business.

We've seen that your record label may be able to reimburse or provide you with an advance that you can use to pay certain touring and other costs, but they will not cover all your expenses. I have listed below some examples of the types of expenditure you are likely to incur throughout the course of your career or while you are actively making and performing your music:

Recording costs: producer/engineer fees, studio hire costs, digital storage, equipment rental, guest musician fees, mastering fees.

Promotional costs: graphic artist, marketing plan, publicist fees, promotion fees, flyers and posters, photographer fees, social media costs.

Business team costs: personal manager commissions, business manager fees, booking agent or publicist commissions.

Office expenses: rent, stationery, postage, phone and utilities, computer costs.

Equipment costs: instrument purchases/rentals, tour luggage, equipment maintenance (e.g. strings and drumsticks, recording and playback equipment, mixers, sound system, rehearsal space costs.

Songwriting costs: song registration and filing costs; Performance Right Society costs, lessons, study/research expenses (i.e. music you buy), conferences or seminars.

Legal & professional fees: music consultant fees, publicist fees and lawyer fees, tax advice.

Touring costs: van rental/purchase, insurance costs, flights, bus, train tickets, fuel, per diem (for food, lodging etc.), tour manager, lighting, sound equipment.

Accounting fees: tour accountant, bookkeeping, financial statement preparation and preparing tax returns, tax planning advice, royalty auditing fees.

Merchandise costs: t-shirt design costs, manufacturing and shipping, legal document fees.

Miscellaneous expenses: costumes/stage clothing, insurance, trade magazine subscriptions.

Commissions

Commissions are fees earned by your manager, booking agents, lawyers and business managers and are common place in the music industry. Artists usually formalise such agreements by way of written contract.

There are typically two types of deals; applying an agreed rate (i.e. percentage) to either your gross income or your net income. Gross refers to your total income before any costs are deducted. Net refers to the amount of income remaining after certain costs have been deducted.

The major area of controversy in relation to the negotiation of commission rates relates to earnings from live performances. While many managers still insist upon charging the agreed rate of commission on the gross income, most managers now accept that this is unfair. Although a lengthy tour might generate substantial gross income, the costs associated with the tour mean that the actual profits of the tour are very small. For example, if your tour grosses £100,000 and you have tour costs of £80,000, you will be left with £20,000 profit. If you were on a gross deal of 20% with your manager, the entirety of the £20,000 will be paid over to them with nothing left in the bank for you or your band. On the other hand, if you had agreed a 20% net deal with your manager, you would pay over £4,000 to your manager and have £16,000 to share amongst your band.

A manager will invariably require reimbursement of their expenses. This should extend only to the expenses incurred by the manger specifically on behalf of the artist. The manager's overhead costs should not be recoverable from you. It's useful to have a right of approval for expenses incurred by your manager above a particular financial limit.

The lifeblood of any business is its ability to collect cash and pay bills, particularly when it comes to its owners having enough funds to cover ongoing expenses. I have seen occasions when artists are extremely profitable, but they do not have enough operating capital to meet their needs. Consequently, they may be forced to lower their show fees and play more often to make up for the cash shortfall. This can lead to negative 'knock on' effects such as 'burning out' and 'overplaying' which can ultimate reduce the demand for your music.

One of the most significant factors to be considered in your cash management is the timing of your income, i.e. knowing exactly when it should be hitting your bank account. Once you are comfortable with the cash receipt side of your business and the timing of the collections of funds from your sales, it is necessary to consider the expenses and other cash needs. The same rule applies to costs as it does to income. You need to make sure you have a handle on the type of costs you are likely to incur, how much they are going to be and when you will need to pay them.

The more effort that you put into forecasting cash the more accurately you will be able to predict the resources needed for your music business. The ability to predict cash resources is an art and is by no means a well-defined science, but a professional advisor who has experience within the music industry can add enormous value to this process. In the next chapter, I will introduce you to the people who make up your professional business team.

PART IV: CHOOSING YOUR TEAM

There are a number of key players who make up your professional business team, each with their own roles and areas of expertise.

For the purpose of this book I will refer to your professional business team to mean your accountant, business manager or tax advisor. Of course, there are many other professionals who drive the more commercial aspects of your business, such as your manager, agent and lawyer. First of all, let's make some distinctions between these professionals.

Your personal manager helps you with your major business decisions, such as deciding which record company or publisher to sign with, how much to ask for, getting you the best deals with promoters and agents, and helping you with the creative process, like deciding which songs to record and producers to work with. Your agents will be arranging and negotiating show fees with promoters, and your lawyer will be the one scrutinizing and advising you of the important legal implications of the contracts you enter into.

As mentioned earlier on in the book, it can be helpful to see your professional business team as your first line of defence. When it comes to artists choosing their professional business team I am often staggered to see that many are hiring family members to take care of business for them. I have seen this to be very dangerous as most of them aren't qualified to do the job, and even when they are, it's difficult for them to be totally objective about you even if they do have your best interests at heart. Also, do you want family members knowing what you spent your money on last summer in Vegas (it could lead to an interesting dinner conversation)? Can you imagine how awkward it would be firing them if they did a bad job? How do you decide how much to pay them? From my experience of seeing artists held back by working with family, I would strongly recommend that you don't hire them unless you have an extremely good reason.

On the point of hiring friends and family as part of your business team, I have experienced the tricky scenario occur where an inexperienced personal manager maintains control of the finances and business affairs of their artist. It was clear from the start of our working relationship that there was some tomfoolery going on with the artist's business matters, as his management team was extremely reluctant to hand over financial records (as required by accountants when taking on new clients) and they were very cagey and defensive in our initial meeting with them. When we asked the artist directly about his business structure and affairs he simply explained to us that he was unconcerned as he whole heartedly trusted his childhood friend to look after his businesses—he had always been the 'business savvy' one after all. We took a closer look at what was going on. It wasn't good. It turned out his manager was paying himself 25% of all the artists' earnings (their agreement was 15%), and the business was showing some very unusual expense claims. They had also been fiddling the VAT returns, exposing the artist to the serious position of potentially defrauding the government. The artist had no idea what had been going on but had wondered why he didn't have much cash to live on—but he was reluctant to rock the boat as this was supposedly his friend. We soon intervened for him, but the lesson here is to pay attention to your business affairs, particularly if you delegate these duties to inexperienced people. If you do decide to have people with personal connections to you to help you manage and run your business, it is always prudent to have an independent, objective third party advisor take a look at your numbers at regular intervals to be sure that nothing is being overlooked.

Why is my professional business team important?

Who you choose to advise and manage your business affairs can mean the difference between a long and successful career and being left penniless. If you pick the right people, you can set the logistical details of your career on autopilot and check up on your business affairs only periodically. That said, if you set to autopilot and pick the wrong people to advise and run your music business then there could be chaos! Financial disasters can come from hiring someone who is a crook, or they can come from an honest person, with the best of intentions, but with the lack of expertise, drive or time to support your business.

Your business team is important because they:

1. Safeguard your wealth
2. Keep you on the right side of the law
3. Save you time and money
4. Can generate you additional income
5. Provide you with a great sounding board

1. Safeguarding your wealth

Your professional business team has a fiduciary and legal duty to protect your money. They are often managing your bank accounts, collecting your earnings, making payments, negotiating contracts and making sure you are not overpaying your taxes.

Having someone scrutinizing and evaluating your business transactions adds a layer of security and comfort knowing that someone in your wider music team is not taking you for a ride. After all, your professional advisors are there to sit on your side of the table—they don't work for your manager!

2. Keeping you on the right side of the law

Your professional business team is also responsible for making sure you stay on the right side of the law in respect to your business affairs. Registering with the tax authorities for social security, filing accounts and tax returns are some examples of the work they undertake to help you fulfil your legal business requirements.

Although your professional advisors can help you with making sure all your legal and tax filings are in hand, it is ultimately your responsibility to file your tax returns, accounts and adhere to your duties as a company director (only, of course, if you are the director).

3. *Save you time and money*

Consider for a moment the value of your own time: how much more valuable could your time be if you spent it writing, recording or touring, particularly if during this time you create a hit record?

I've come across a lot of clients who have been preparing their own tax returns for years. One particular artist was quite comfortable with numbers—at the time he managed a music venue and promoted various club nights on the side, so dealing with finances and accounting for money was second nature to him. Eventually his band started taking off, and his time to attend to these matters quickly diminished so he got in touch with me.

At our first meeting two things became immediately clear—he had been significantly overpaying is tax over the last 5 years by not claiming all the deductions he was entitled to, and his tax returns were not accurately declaring his income and personal circumstances. I was quickly able to remedy the situation by refiling his tax returns and securing a big tax refund in the process. The point I'm trying to make here is that he was extremely busy and trying to juggle many jobs, so his tax returns didn't get the attention they required, and he ended up paying much more money in taxes than he had to because he didn't have the tricks and tools up his sleeve that accountants have.

Before taking on the burden of doing your accounts and taxes yourself ask the following:

Is this a good use of my time?
Do I have the expertise to do this properly?
What is at stake if I get things wrong?

Let's say it takes you 10 hours to do your taxes, and your time is worth £100 an hour. That's a cost of £1,000 to do your taxes yourself. And there's always the risk you've made errors. Imagine what you could have done with that 10 hours (if you had it to spare in the first place). If you would have written or developed a successful song in this time, then that time would have been worth substantially more than £1,000 to you.

Here's another way of looking at it—if you wanted to professionally record a song to release you would not likely master it yourself. You would have an expert do it or someone with the best reputation for mastering music in your genre because it gives the record the best chance of being successful. As with anything, hiring the right professional will help you to get the best results.

If you have someone else do the administrative tasks, like bookkeeping and your taxes, you'll not only have extra time free to concentrate on writing songs and generating revenue, but you'll have the peace of mind that an expert is taking care of the details.

An accountant will complete the appropriate forms for you and return them on time to the appropriate authority in order and on time, leaving you free to focus on earning more money.

So let's assume time isn't an issue and you're 100% confident you know how to complete all of those forms correctly. Perhaps you have a computer program that does it for you. Completing the forms correctly is one thing, but doing them in a way that's going to save you the most money is another. A good advisor will make sure you take full advantage of every legal way to minimize your tax bill, assuming that's what you want, of course.

There will come a point in your life when you decide that you want to buy a house. In my experience, this will involve obtaining a mortgage for the majority of you. For many people in the UK who are self-employed or run their own businesses it is extremely tricky to persuade the bank to lend money. This also extends to lending to music artists, for whom mortgage lenders will need some extra persuasion. This is because the banks view lending to you as more risky than someone who has a contract of employment, for example. People who have a regular job are guaranteed the same income each month and notice periods in contracts mean that there is less risk that they will fall behind on their mortgages.

Income for artists can be lumpy and unpredictable at best. Many artists who are in a position to buy a house will, more often than not, have complex business structures which can be extremely difficult to communicate to mortgage lenders on their own, and of course the bank will always have lots of questions to ask you before they handover the money. This is where your business adviser comes in handy. They will be able to communicate your business structure, past and future earnings and asset position to them in a way that bankers can understand. Banks will also take more comfort from information provided by other professionals as financial professionals have a duty of care when providing information to them.

4. *Generating you additional income*

There are some very clever business managers, accountants and tax advisors out there who have the experience and 'know how' to help grow the value of your music rights, help with negotiations on business deals and even make 'money spinning' introductions through their professional network.

Clever accountants can structure contracts in certain ways to maximize earnings and reduce tax. They may also be better positioned than your lawyer or manager to advise you on the financial aspects of contracts. Given that they are in the numbers business, I would always recommend that your accountant reviews financial arrangements found in any agreements before you sign them.

5. Provide you with a great sounding board

As well as doing all the paperwork and minimizing your tax bill—your professional business team can also be a great source of advice to help you grow your music business and navigate any problems and concerns you have along the way.

In order for your business to be a success it's important that you make the correct financial management decisions early on as you lay the foundation of your business. A few wrong moves in the early days could be disastrous for your career. Your professional business team will be there as a sounding board for your business and commercial ideas. They know your career potential almost as well as you do and should, of course, know the financial side a lot better than you. Objective input from someone who knows your business but doesn't have the emotional attachment can be priceless.

In addition to being a great sounding board for larger business decisions, understanding what costs can be deducted from income and what can't is an extremely important tool for the accountant, and there are many tricks that good accountants know about to maximize the costs you can deduct from income, ultimately reducing your tax and saving you more of those £'s. As we have seen in Part 1, more money can be put into your pocket by saving an additional £1 rather than earning another £1 of income, and given your tax bill is likely to be your biggest expense in the year, minimising your tax seriously pays off.

In my experience, the differences between a business manager, accountant and tax adviser have been a source of enormous confusion and misunderstanding. Many industry stalwarts I speak to still have trouble telling them apart and yet it is crucial to be able to distinguish the roles in order to allocate responsibilities so that your team works well together, takes advantage of each individual's strengths and to ensure that all important matters are properly handled. I'll now talk through their roles and what you can expect from each.

The Business Manager

The business manager is the person who looks after your money. He or she collects it, keeps track of it, pays your bills, invests it and coordinates filing your tax returns.

The term 'business manager' originated in the US, where it is commonly used in the entertainment industry. Your business manager works alongside your personal manager and booking agent. Personal managers tend to make the major business decisions and look after the day-to-day creative aspects of your career, whereas business managers take responsibility for running your businesses.

In the US, the objective of the business manager is to oversee your finances in order to maximize your earning potential. A business manager will make sure you are paid promptly, he or she will check your bills and invoices to make sure they accurately reflect expenses and then make payments on behalf of your business and sometimes in respect of your personal financial affairs. It is their job to set budgets, handle investments, and represent you when dealing with tax and legal matters.

Sometimes business managers are also in charge of the financial aspects of a tour. If this is the case they will set budgets and calculate whether the tour will be profitable. Once the tour is in motion they will arrange for your production team and crew to be paid and ensure performance fees are collected from the promoters. It is their job to monitor the tour closely and to warn people if it looks as if it will go over budget.

In the UK, it is more common for high-profile touring bands to hire a tour accountant or engage a specialist music accounting firm to provide the same tour accounting services as a business manager would do in the US.

A number of disciplines are involved in accounting. At its root is bookkeeping. Your business manager should also be a capable bookkeeper. A bookkeeper will keep track of all the money that a business handles, including money paid to the business, money paid out, and assets the business holds. His or her goal is to keep the books of the company balanced so that anyone can assess, at a glance, the financial state of the company. As an established artist you may have a number of companies that you personally own and are responsible for, so a business manager has to co-ordinate payments and contracts accurately between the various entities, which will require someone with a high degree of competence and organizational skills.

In the UK, the term 'business manager' is regarded slightly differently. They still provide day-to-day support for your business administration, such as paying your bills, sending out invoices, and dealing with other ad hoc personal and business financial matters. They are the point of contact between you and your accountant or tax adviser, but they also work closely with accountants and tax advisors to make sure you are on the right track. Usually, music and entertainment accounting practices in the UK have a business management department.

Perhaps the main difference between the role of the business manager in the UK and the US is that business managers in the US tend to be more hands on and more involved in some of the commercial business decision making. They also get paid differently in the US.

Business managers generally get paid a lot more in the US, and it is common for them to take 5% of an artist's earnings which reflects, to a certain extent, the increased commercial role they play in an artists' business like negotiating deals. This is rarely the case in the UK and they are usually paid an hourly rate for their services, which is common for many professional service firms in the UK. Business managers in their own right are much less common in the UK and tend to be predominantly seen in entertainment practices or as a special service to the ultra-rich.

For many years, a number of accountants in the UK have resisted marketing themselves as business managers, probably because many are chartered accountants (who are a very proud people having spent many years training in order to call themselves a 'chartered accountant'). However, the reality is that many business management services in the UK fall under the remit of an accountant in one way or another, and so, they provide these services alongside their more specialist services, as I will discuss next.

A point worth mentioning here is that there are no barriers to entry in becoming a business manager, accountant or tax advisor, which I find terrifying. You have to be especially careful that the person who ends up looking after your finances is experienced enough and has had the required training.

The accounting profession has, of course, worked hard to remedy this lack of consistent accreditation over the years through the creation of regulatory bodies like the Institute of Chartered Accountants in England & Wales (ICAEW), The Association of Chartered Certified Accountants (ACCA) and the Chartered Institute of Taxation (CIOT). People who are members of these institutions will have demonstrated they have expert knowledge, work experience and are held to the highest professional and ethical standards. In this book I will refer to these people as 'qualified' accountants.

The Accountant

An accountant is one of the main players in any business and is one of the oldest professions in the world; businesses have been practicing accounting for thousands of years. Essentially, your accountant monitors and records the flow of money through your business.

It is their responsibility to verify the accuracy of all money transactions recorded by bookkeepers and business managers, for example, and to make sure that all these transactions are legal and follow current guidelines.

It may be that an accountant works for your business on a contractual basis to do the books or tax returns, or you may hire one to help you with your financial decisions and other money-related issues. Your accountant is the person who advises you as to the most appropriate business structure you should have in place. They are often the people responsible for preparing your business accounts and filing your personal and business tax returns.

The term "accountant" is not regulated, so anyone can call themselves an accountant regardless of their background, experience, training or professional qualifications. Like any industry profession, there can be cowboys or people who don't have the ability to advise clients on all aspects of accountancy and taxation. If the accountant gets it wrong it will be their client who ends up in trouble. This can result in HMRC imposing fines, penalties and at the very worst–a prison sentence on the client. This is not to say that all the best accountants are qualified, but having a suitably 'qualified accountant' who adheres to professional and ethical codes of conduct should provide you with some peace of mind. Examples of qualified accountants are those who are members of recognized accountancy bodies, such as:

- Institute of Chartered Accountants in England & Wales (ACA or FCA)
- Institute of Chartered Accountants of Scotland (CA)
- Institute of Chartered Accountants in Ireland (ICAI)
- Association of Chartered Certified Accountants (ACCA or FCCA)
- Chartered Institute of Management Accountants (ACMA or FCMA)
- Chartered Institute of Public Finance and Accountancy (CPFA)
- Association of International Accountants (AIAA or FAIA)
- Association of Accounting Technicians (MAAT or FMAAT)

As with many professions, accounting is segmented into different types of accountants depending on the various roles they offer to businesses. These range from accounting technicians to public accountants and auditors. It takes a minimum of three years of rigorous exams and professional work experience to become a chartered accountant, which requires one to demonstrate continued professional development each year. This means they should be able to show they are up to date with changes in legislation in their particular field of expertise. Hiring someone who is a chartered accountant would be a good starting point in selecting your accountant but is by no means the only thing to consider.

As with many professions, accountants can have their own areas of specialty within their profession. They may specialize in personal tax, VAT, limited company accounts or even accounting systems. Going more in depth, accountants will specialize depending on what industry and type of clients they have experience working with. Their clients may primarily consist of owner-run businesses that sell car parts, for example, or in my case, artists running their businesses in the music industry. You should always be wary of choosing an accountant who has little or no experience working in the music sector. Each industry has its own complexities, which can often take many years to master.

Even when working within the music industry itself, the challenges and specialisms can be broken down further. Some music industry accountants may have more experience working with DJ/Producers rather than metal rock bands. As an example, DJs tend to travel relatively light and therefore can play in many international territories over a short space of time, meaning they will need an accountant with broad international experience. Additionally, some major international DJs have residency agreements with major night clubs, which means a different approach would be needed to tax planning compared to metal bands that generally have higher production costs, fewer key territories and more band members to split the profits between.

Costly mistakes could be made by an accountant with a lack of experience in dealing with someone with your set of circumstances, even though decisions may be made with the best of intentions. Also, opportunities could be missed if your accountant is unaware of industry protocols or does not have a clear understanding of the various challenges facing you throughout your career.

Accountants play a very important role in your business, and if they are doing their job well, they will be adding enormous value to your business. More often than not accountants are seen as a necessary evil: to look after those annoying administrative burdens like filing accounts and tax returns on time. Instead, you should see them as your key business partner. They should be one of your closest advisers and should be there to support you when things are going well and more importantly, when things aren't going so well.

The Tax Advisor

A tax advisor is a financial expert with training in tax laws. They serve businesses and individuals alike by staying current on new tax law and ensuring you are in the most optimal tax position.

Anyone can be a tax advisor, but tax is an extremely complex area of law and administration, so I recommend you that you hire a tax advisor who is a member of a professional body, such as the Chartered Institute of Taxation. Admission to membership of the Chartered Institute of Taxation is widely regarded as one of the toughest professional qualifications that require members to have passed a number of challenging exams and demonstrate three years of professional experience on top of existing professional qualifications, such as being a lawyer or a chartered accountant.

A tax advisor typically expands the role of the accountant but there can also be some crossover in the services they provide. Often your accountant and tax advisor will work together on your behalf and many larger accounting firms have specialist tax divisions within their firm. They give advice on tax planning, but tax planning isn't done just before the end of the year—it continues throughout the year. You should be talking to your tax advisor at strategic points during the year–every quarter, at a minimum, to discuss strategies for minimizing your taxes—legitimately, of course!

Your tax advisor will probably also prepare your business tax return and personal tax return. However, many accountants can also prepare and file your tax returns. After your tax return is filed, there may still be work for your tax advisor to do if you get audited or the tax authorities come knocking at your door. Your tax advisor should have a good reputation within the tax profession and the experience to deal with any potential questions from the tax authorities, as well as the negotiation skills to get the best results on your tax position.

A good tax advisor should also be able to clearly communicate tax law and strategies to you in a way that is accessible and easy for you to understand. To summarise, tax advisors typically perform the following duties:

- Strategize with you to minimize your tax liability
- Communicate and explain tax issues to you
- Prepare your tax returns
- Keep you compliant with your tax obligations
- Negotiate with the tax authorities on your behalf

What services do I need and when do I need them?

Hiring the right business professional will make life easier for you at each step. That doesn't mean you always need to employ a bookkeeper, business manager or accountant full time or hire one on a monthly or retainer basis. Sometimes just a couple of hours of their time will be enough. However, it is best to seek out an accountant or business manager sooner rather than later since most accountants prefer to have a clean slate to work from. It can be very time consuming and costly to undo any mistakes that have been made in the past, and getting things right from the start is much more rewarding and will add value for everyone.

Nevertheless, you should not rush into signing up with a business manager, accountant or tax advisor. It is better to wait until you find the right one rather than engaging the wrong one. Your accountant will be one of your most trusted and key advisors on your team and throughout your career your relationship with them will be a very personal one since they will know your financial affairs and goals intimately. Of course, if the relationship with your accountant does break down or you realise that you have made a mistake in hiring them there is nothing stopping you from changing advisors.

So what are the moments in your life as an artist that you do not want to miss out on by hiring an accountant to help you rather than doing the work yourself? I'll talk you through some of these critical situations now.

You'll need advice about your businesses' legal structure before you start

Once you have established you have a business, you should seek professional advice from an accountant or tax advisor.

Your career has the potential to take off extremely quickly so it's important to plan and have the correct structure in place before it does because you cannot go back and retrospectively change it to something that is more beneficial to you.

Not all businesses have the same legal structure – there are different types that are determined by a number of factors. We have briefly discussed the most common trading structures in the UK (see Part I): limited companies, limited liability partnerships or sole traders. Again, each option should be carefully evaluated by an expert using accurate information on your current financial circumstances and future aspirations.

You'll need help with your business administration

Once you have carefully decided on the best business structure and had your accountant set this up for you, the next step will be to think about getting some expert help with handling the day-to-day financial administration of your business.

It's great if you are able to record and keep track of all income and expenses yourself to start with, as this will certainly save you some money in the short term. However, things can quickly become complex and time consuming if you do it on your own. If you feel like you're losing control of who owes you money and how much, you will probably need someone to help you get back on track.

A business manager will be able to do this for you, and so will an accountant, but always check how much they will charge for the work, as qualified accountants will charge more than bookkeepers for the same work. If they use cloud-based accounting software, they'll be able to share your business accounts with you quickly and easily. They will also be able to produce tables and charts that will help you to understand your company's financial position at a glance. This will help you monitor the pulse of your business and keep track of important things like cash flow. Cash flow is the bloodline of a business—if you have more money going out than you have coming in, things aren't going to work out well for you. Having a business manager who can anticipate costs and time investments properly, so they align with the timing of your income, can make the difference of having a well-run business and one which goes belly up. Especially in the music industry, when cash flow is more erratic than most businesses and more difficult to predict, you need someone on your team who is experienced at keeping a close eye on how much money is coming in and going out.

When you are ready to delegate

No doubt one of the things you like best is control. But sometimes it can stop you from delegating. As you become more in demand as an artist you will feel more and more overworked, spending many long days in the studio, travelling, and regularly playing late shows.

You might feel that no one can possibly know your business as well as you do, and therefore nobody can handle any part of your business as well as you can. An inability to delegate can mean you're left feeling overworked and stressed. At some point you will have to let go and learn to trust other people to handle some parts of the business so that you can look after the rest.

The most successful business owners in the world are experts at delegating work to the right people – so try and learn from them and learn when it's time to let go.

Get help when you have to deal with the government

Dealing with government paperwork can be a daunting experience, especially when all you really care about is your music. This is why so many artists tend to hire an accountant just before their first tax filing is due or when they get a threatening demand from the tax authorities through the post.

But accountants can also help you cope with more than just tax returns. They can help you interact with the government in other ways:

- Complete and file the legal and compliance documents for your business
- Keep you up to date with latest tax laws
- Prepare annual financial accounts
- Keep your company's status updated in the government's company register
- Maintain records of directors and other administrative personnel
- Organize and record share and business ownership allocation, such as when a new business is formed, when a band member leaves or a new band member joins
- Handle your payroll and ensuring that all employees' tax codes and payments are recorded correctly

Preparing your tax documents correctly could save you money – perhaps more money than your accountant or tax advisor charges you. And a good accountant will use their knowledge of tax laws and legislation to suggest ways you can free up cash flow, save money and raise capital for other business or charitable enterprises you have in mind.

Get help in case you get an audit or tax inspection

As an artist starting out it's statistically unlikely you will get audited because there are so many small businesses and relatively few government auditors. But as your business empire grows you will become more exposed to government authorities. As you move into their radar they will take more and more of an interest in your business affairs. If you do get a tax inspection or tax audit it can be very expensive, stressful and time consuming.

If you don't have an accountant or tax advisor at this point, it's a good time to hire one. They can give you advice on how to work within the auditing or tax investigation process. They can also help ensure you don't violate any tax laws afterwards – because the government will almost certainly be watching you.

But it's better to hire an accountant before an audit or tax investigation ever happens, especially if you can find one who will offer audit or tax investigation insurance. This covers the fees you would have had to pay if you needed to respond to an official enquiry, review, investigation or audit by a tax department, such as from HM Revenue & Customs. Getting tax investigation insurance from your accountant can be a huge plus as it means they won't charge any extra for the considerable amount of work they'll have to carry out during the audit process.

As you can see, business managers, accountants and tax advisors can help you during every stage of your businesses' development. That doesn't mean you *have* to hire one, but the right advisor should make life easier for you and improve your financial position, so that you can concentrate on what you love doing for as long as possible.

Tips for Selecting the Right Individuals for Your Team

Sometimes your manager will help you build your professional business team. They are most likely to recommend someone they have liked working with the past and know that they will do a good job of making sure you are looked after, and importantly to them, their commissions are calculated accurately and paid on time. You should certainly listen to your manager as the good ones will have an excellent network of professional advisors, and of course they will be looking out for your best interests.

It's worth pointing out here that the experience they had with an accountant may not be the same as the experience you have with the same accountant. Just as in every other aspect of life, some personalities get on better than others. So be cautious in writing off advisors your manager may not get on with on a personal level and be sure to ask them why they haven't recommended someone, particularly if you've heard good things and would like to work with them.

You should always ask your manager to recommend someone who doesn't already act for them on their personal and business matters. Usually, your manager will not introduce you to their personal accountant as this could result in a conflict of interest. As a professional, an accountant is unlikely to take you on or act as your advisor if they also advise your manager, agent or lawyer. After all, your accountant should be sitting on your side of the table on all matters and occasionally this could include disputes on management commission, which is a conversation you want handled with complete objectivity.

There are other ways to find and shortlist candidates for your professional business team, the most obvious of which is searching the internet and asking your industry contacts if they can make any recommendations, or if they've had any positive experiences. Company websites are a good starting point for getting a feel for the business; are they a dynamic firm that understands the concerns of artists or are they the traditional accounting practice promising a steady hand? Another good way to start reducing your shortlist is to visit the LinkedIn profiles of some of the names recommended to you. LinkedIn is used by most accountants to connect with other professionals, and there you'll be able to easily review professional recommendations and gauge the experience of the people rather than simply what services the business offers, which is often all you'll get from an accountant's website.

Whichever approach you take, you should be proactive in finding your trusted business advisor and you should set about compiling a short list of candidates. To help you with this, I have compiled some questions to help you decide, some of which you'll need to ask when you set up your first introduction meeting with them.

- How experienced are you?
- Will I be invited to pick up the phone and call you if there is a problem?
- Do you work with other music artists and in what capacities?
- How have you established your reputation and what are your reputed strengths?
- Are you primarily a business manager, accountant or tax specialist?
- How can you help me throughout my career?
- What services can you provide, i.e. bookkeeping, statutory accounts, personal and corporate tax returns, international tax administration, tour accounting?
- Are you a qualified business professional i.e. a chartered accountant or chartered tax advisor and are you regulated?
- Do you have experience working with international artists?
- Do you have the experience to represent me when I become a superstar?
- How will you handle negotiating contracts on my behalf?
- Where are you based and how easy will you be to access?
- How much time will you be able to spend on my affairs?
- Why do you want to work with me, specifically?
- Will you be able to deal efficiently with returning phone calls and email correspondence?
- Do you have a history of working with successful artists?
- Are you able to provide references from your existing clients?
- What reports will you be able to provide me, are they easily understandable and how often will I get them? Can I see an example of the reports you generate?
- How much do you charge and what is the monetary value you can add?

Fees

It's quite old fashioned now for professional service firms (such as accountants) to charge based on the time they spend providing the service to you. Accountants and other professionals (lawyers in particular) have been loyal to this method of pricing for many years now. This price structure is actually based on Karl Marx's theory (the father of Communism) that the value of a commodity is solely determined by the labour inputs that go into it. I may ruffle a few old feathers here, but in my opinion the value of anything in this world is solely determined by the person who pays for it, especially when it comes to the music industry. Digitalization of the music industry drove down costs and increased efficiency and music discovery—all driven by what the music consumer wanted.

The primary questions you are looking for an answer to regarding pricing are likely the following: how much should I be paying my accountant, and how do I know if I'm getting ripped off? I cannot answer this with certainty because research shows that there is no set market price for accounting services in the UK. This throws the Karl Marx concept of cost plus pricing (this is what accountants call it) out the window. Today, accounting services are not seen as a commodity (i.e. something that has a market price) — you are not buying just the product and service (set of accounts or tax return), but you are also buying the advisor behind the service too. This is something that cannot be bought anywhere else. The best advisors recognize that they cannot work with everyone and price their services based on the value they can bring to the table rather that how many hours they can spend advising them. In other words, the higher the value an accountant can offer your business, the more money and time they will save you and the more money they will likely charge. While this is not true in every case, as a professional in the industry for many years, I can assure you that most music business professionals are worth what they charge, meaning you will quite likely get more value for an accountant who charges more.

From your point of view, I'm sure you'd prefer your accountant or lawyer, for example, to tell you how much their fees will be upfront, rather than being hit with a surprise bill that ended up being a lot more than you expected. One very troubling aspect to the price per hour billing structure is the validity of asking the question: how do you know that they have accurately recorded the time spent doing the work? I recommend that you always agree the fees up front when you can as it transfers the risk from you back onto your accountant as they now have to work efficiently to meet the fee agreement. You have transferred the risk in two ways; you know that you will not be charged more when the work is complete and you can manage your cash flow much better seeing as you know how much you need to pay and when you need to pay it.

Some final considerations on your professional advisors

Be wary that some advisors have a big mouth. Although it may appear impressive when they discuss with you their list of clients, be especially careful of those who tell you about other people's lives. It means they are most probably telling other people about you. Do you really want someone who knows every aspect of your business and personal financials to be spreading the good, the bad and the ugly about your successes and failures throughout the industry? I think not. Confidentiality, professionalism and integrity are all key traits to look for in your professional advisor. It's actually not a bad idea to ask for personal information when interviewing prospective advisors to see what they are willing to disclose.

A little story that I like to tell my clients when helping them to get a perspective on fees and value goes as follows: a captain of a large container ship notices that something isn't right below deck and it's beginning to fill with water very quickly. The situation is serious as they are transporting some incredibly valuable cargo and of course the safety of the crew is in jeopardy. The costs of the ship going down will run in to millions of pounds and of course you can't put a value on the potential lives lost. No one on board can identify the problem so they call upon an expert on a nearby ship as a last resort to save the ship from going under.

The captain leads the expert, an old, shy man, below deck and shows him where the problem is. The old man takes a few minutes to look around and carefully feels along the antiquated pipes before getting a wooden mallet out of his bag. He then gently taps at the pipe. Suddenly the pipe makes a chugging sound, and the water pump comes back to life, slowly reducing the water level in the engine room. Problem solved.

They both make their way back up towards the top deck, and the captain can't thank the old man enough for saving his crew and cargo. When presented with the bill, the captain is shocked to see that he has charged £10,000 for 5 minutes work. "That surely can't be right!" grumbles the captain. "How did you come up with that figure?"

The old man calmly responds, "well...that's easy...I consider it fair that I charge £50 as I had to pick the right tool and I carry it with me...and £9,950 for knowing exactly where to tap on the pipe."

In truth, the value to the captain is exponentially more than the £10,000 paid to the old man to save the ship. What I am trying to demonstrate here is that having someone who knows exactly what to do to keep you afloat and when to do it is incredibly valuable, irrespective of the time it takes to do a certain task.

Finally, make sure you can see what *value* each member of your team brings to the table and ensure they can justify this against the fees you pay them. In the case of the story above, I believe the £10,000 fee for 5 minutes of work is fully justifiable.

PART V: UNDERSTANDING THE NUMBERS

Ok, so financial reports are not sexy or glamorous and you will certainly not be alone if your eyes glaze over when they are put in front of you. So I won't show you one here. I will instead put one as far away as possible from the rest of the information here (examples are in the back of this book) so you can use as reference or take a look should the mood take you.

Why are financial reports important to me?

Can you imagine going on a long car journey without the benefit of the instruments on your dashboard telling you your speed, how much fuel you have left and the temperature? Of course not. Just as these instruments are critical when undertaking long car journeys, so financial reports are essential for monitoring your journey through your music career.

Financial reports come in different forms and are compiled for different reasons depending on the need they fulfil. For example, your manager may need monthly reports showing your earnings so that they can calculate the commissions that are due, your record label may need reports showing your expenses so that they can pay your tour support fees and you will need end of year business accounts to calculate the amount of tax you need to pay and to comply with the law.

As an accountant, I see huge value in organizing and having access to key financial information. After all, it's my job to use this information to help my clients make decisions. Here are some of the ways I use my clients' financial reports:

They are a scorecard – I get a buzz whenever I see my clients beat their previous results and I always strive to help them improve on their previous years' records. We all like to visualize our successes, and financial reports are the main vehicle for measuring our business and personal financial performances over time.

They provide a financial health check – They provide vital information about your businesses' financial health. I compile statements based on day-to-day bookkeeping that tracks money flowing in and out of the business, so I know how much cash you have now and what your position would be months or even a year from now.

They are useful for decision making – The information in the statements offers benchmarks and feedback that can help you make minor adjustments to your business and also its overall direction. They are useful for helping you to plan your future, whether that be a family holiday, a new car or buying a house.

In the next section, I'll introduce to some of the key reports and concepts behind them and how you can use them to your advantage.

What do financial reports show?

There are three widely-used financial reports that will be relevant to your music business, and understanding their role in your business and how you can base critical financial decisions from the information they disclose will be key to your financial success as a music artist.

1. Profit and Loss: reports on your income, expenses and profits over a period of time

2. Balance Sheet: reports on your business assets, liabilities and equity of a business at a given point in time
3. Cash Flow Statement: provides information regarding your cash receipts and cash payments over a period of time or into the future

Profit and Loss

By having a regular profit and loss report for your business (at least quarterly or monthly), you will be able to:

- Answer the question, "How much money am I making, if any?"
- Compare your projected performance with past performance. "Have I earned more money on this leg of the tour compared with the same leg last year?"
- Compare your performance against industry benchmarks. "Are we paying more for our tour manager compared with other artists with a similar profile to ours?"
- Use past performance trends to form reasonable forecasts for the future. "If we expect to earn the same as last year, will I be able to buy a house this year?"
- Show your business growth and financial health over time. "Has the value of my brand increased from last year to this year?"
- Detect any problems regarding sales, margins and expenses within a reasonable timeframe so adjustments may be made to recoup losses or decrease expenses. "Is our manager taking their commission on gross income rather than net of expenses as per the agreement?"
- Provide proof of income if you need a loan or mortgage. "Can I show the bank that I have been earning consistently over the last 3 years and will continue to do so in the future?"
- Calculate your income and expenses when completing and submitting your tax returns.

Balance Sheet

In contrast to the profit and loss account, the balance sheet is a statement detailing what a business owns (assets) and owes (liabilities) and the value of the owner's equity (or net worth of the business) at a specific point in time. The balance sheet is also known as a statement of financial position because it shows a summary of the business's financial position.

A balance sheet enables you to:

- Quickly see the financial strengths and capabilities of your business.
- Review the level of assets, debt and working capital of your business.
- Compare the increase or decrease in the value of your business overtime.
- See the relative liquidity of your business. "Do I have assets I can sell quickly?"
- Analyse your ability to pay all short-term and long-term debts as they come due.
- Review the composition of assets and liabilities, the relative proportions of debt and equity financing and the amount of retained earnings (investors find all this information very useful).

Cash Flow

A cash flow report is important to you because it can be used to assess the timing, amount and predictability of future income and costs, and as such, it can be considered a reliable resource to use as the basis for budgeting. A cash flow report can answer the questions, "where did my money come from?" and "where did it go?"

For your music business, it is probably one of the most important reports as it traces the flow of money into or out of your business. A cash flow statement should be prepared as frequently as possible (either monthly or quarterly) so that you can make sure you have enough income coming in to cover your costs. It also acts as a tool for identifying which costs you need to reduce or delay paying to make sure you don't go into the red. Strategic business cash flow management involves knowing which bills are the most logical ones on which to postpone payment, based on your cash flow needs, and taking advantage of these opportunities when necessary.

It's great if you can understand a little about what your financial reports are showing you, but realise that no one is expecting you to fully understand them. Accountancy is a profession that takes many years of training and experience to comprehend the complexities of financial reporting. It is your accountant's job to prepare your financial reports and provide financial information that is useful to you and in a way that you can easily understand so that they can guide you in your decision making.

What records do I need to keep?

Financial reports require information to be input before they can be prepared. These are taken from the records a business keeps. Making sure you have a system for collecting your income and expenditure is the first important task in the process of sound financial management. Accurate and regular financial information allows you to monitor the success or failure of your business and provides you with information to evaluate the possible consequences of your financial decisions. Regular monitoring of your business activities will help you operate more efficiently, control your cash flow and increase your profitability.

Recording keeping obligations for sole traders (i.e. you are the business)

By law, the UK tax authorities (HM Revenue & Customs) require you to keep your records for at least 5 years after the tax return submission deadline of the relevant tax year. You do not need to submit these records to them but they may ask for them to make sure you're paying the right amount of tax. You need to keep these records for 5 years so that you can show them to the tax authorities if asked.

For example, if you sent your 2015/16 tax return online by 31 January 2017, you must keep records until at least the end of January 2022.

You'll need to keep records of the following:

- All sales and income
- All business expenses
- VAT records if you are registered for VAT
- PAYE records if you employ people
- Records about your personal income

You will need to keep proof of the above by keeping hold of the following:

- All receipts and invoices for your costs
- Bank statements showing the income you have received on the costs that you have paid
- Sales invoices

As well as your standard records, under the traditional accounting method, you'll also need to keep further records to support your tax return which includes details of the following:

- What you are owed but haven't received yet (accountants call these debtors or receivables)
- What you've committed to spend but haven't paid out yet, i.e. what you've received an invoice for but haven't paid yet (accountants call these creditors or payables)
- The value of any stock held at yearend (this could be CDs or merchandise)
- Your end of year bank balances (i.e. bank statements)
- How much you've invested in the business in the year (i.e. investment statements and valuation reports)
- How much money you've taken out for your own use

Record keeping obligations for companies (i.e. a limited company)

If you have a company in your business structure, you are required to keep records about the company itself as well as financial and accounting records. Company records need to be kept longer than for sole traders, which is normally at least 6 years from the end of the last company financial year to which they relate.

You'll need to keep the following details about the company:

- Directors, shareholders and company secretaries
- The results of any shareholder votes and resolutions (formal company agreements etc.)
- Promises of the company to repay loans at a specific date in the future
- Promises the company makes for payments if something goes wrong and it's the company's fault ('indemnities')
- Transactions when someone buys shares in the company
- Loans or mortgages secured against the company's assets

You must also keep accounting records that include the following:

- All money received and spent by the company
- Details of assets owned by the company
- Debts the company owes or is owed
- Stock the company owns at the end of the financial year
- The stock takings you used to work out the stock figure
- All goods brought and sold, and
- Who you bought and sold them to and from
- Receipts, petty cash books, orders and delivery notes
- Sales invoices, contracts, sales books, etc.
- Bank statements and bank correspondence

You *must* make sure your records are accurate. Creating a system for keeping records is a vital part of operating a business. There are many systems available these days with most of them now being electronic and even cloud-based. Each has their advantages and disadvantages and level of technical knowledge required to operate them. Your accountant or bookkeeper can help you determine the best system to fulfil your requirements.

As your career grows, so will the complexity and volume of transactions in your record keeping, therefore please seek help if you are currently handling this yourself and starting to feel overwhelmed.

If you'd like a free copy of an easy-to-operate system for recording your income and expenses then contact me at info@pellartists.com and I'd be happy to send you our free starter pack for artists which includes invoice templates and a specially formatted excel workbook for you to track your income and expenditure.

Do I need to register for VAT?

A common question amongst artists starting out is whether or not they need to register for VAT. If your turnover (total sales) in the previous 12 months exceeds the compulsory registration threshold (£82,000 from 1 April 2015), then yes – you must register. Failure to do so can result in fines. You must also register if you think your business income will exceed the threshold in the year.

If you haven't exceeded the threshold for compulsory registration you can still register voluntarily if it makes sense to do so. If you're a VAT registered business, then you are essentially an unpaid tax collector. You have to add VAT at the appropriate rate to everything you sell (usually at 20%). Note that if you are not registered for VAT you do not need to do this. The additional income you invoice for isn't yours – you're collecting it on behalf of the tax man (HMRC). Every three months you need to pay the tax you've collected over to them.

Now, here's the good bit. When you buy things from other businesses that are registered for VAT (when they charge you VAT), you get to claim this back from the tax man.

So, let's assume that in a 3 month period that you play a show in the UK and your fee is £5,000. If you are registered for VAT you will need to charge an additional £1,000 for VAT, so your total invoice and money collected will be £6,000. In the same period, you also buy some expensive music equipment and spend a lot of money on studio costs and pay a total of £12,000. In this situation, instead of paying money to the tax man at the end of the quarter, they will give you back some money. You will essentially be £1,000 better off than if you hadn't registered for VAT. This is because, although you have to pay £1,000 for the VAT on your income, you can deduct £2,000 from the amount for the VAT on your studio hire costs and music equipment.

Besides the possible financial gain, registering for VAT can improve the perception of your business to the outside world; by not registering for VAT you are effectively telling the world that your music business has income of less than £82,000 each year. If you're trying to present an image of being more established, then not charging VAT would shatter that illusion to those in the know.

It sounds good, right? There are some drawbacks. You need to make sure you carefully manage your cash flow to ensure you can make your payments to the tax man on time. You will also need to regularly report and track all of your business income and expenditures so that you can file your VAT return every three months. As with all areas of tax law, VAT is not always straight-forward. You cannot reclaim VAT on all of your costs. For example, the tax man specifically says you can't reclaim VAT on certain entertaining expenses, and the rules can get complex when you start issuing invoices to people and companies in other countries, so it's well worth getting help from an accountant. Finally, you will also need to factor in the costs of having an accountant prepare and file your VAT returns every three months.

What should I be asking my accountant for?

As previously demonstrated, a good accountant will be able to lead the way when providing information to you. Information is only useful if you can easily understand it, and decisions can be made as a result of digesting the information once it is properly communicated to you.

If you haven't already had these discussions with your accountant, it's time to ask the following questions. And really, if this is the first time you're talking about these things with your accountant, that's a serious problem. And if your accountant can't answer these questions, it's time to hire a new accountant!

How can I improve the financial health of my business?

At the heart of the question, it is about cash flow. You accountant should be proactively helping you to manage your cash flow, finding ways to increase your cash flow and reduce costs.

How can I minimize my income tax?

Your advisor, whether an accountant or tax adviser, needs to be on top of the frequently changing tax laws to help you maximize your financial position. You can benefit enormously by implementing legitimate tax planning strategies.

Of equal importance is the fact that, with the right support, you can be assured that you are meeting all of your tax obligations, thereby avoiding unwanted attention from the tax authorities due to not filing certain accounts and tax returns.

Your advisor should be able to have an informed conversation with you about all the options available to save taxes and protect your business assets as well as your financial longevity.

How can I support my personal goals, such as buying a house?

Your advisor should be able to understand your goals for growth and help you to work towards achieving these goals. A good advisor will help you to identify if you can afford to buy a sports car or a yacht, but more importantly, let you know (in a nice way) when you can't!

We are nearly coming to the end of this short book. In the final chapter I'll be answering some common questions asked by artists starting out.

PART VI: ANSWERING YOUR QUESTIONS

I have sat down with lots of artists just like you over the years and many common questions surface in our initial meetings. Some of these questions I have hoped to address throughout this book—I thought it would be helpful to share a few more questions and answers with you here.

When do I need to file my income tax return?

You will need to file your personal income tax return by 31st January following the end of the tax year. For example, for the period 6th April 2016 to 5th April 2017 you will need to file your tax return (at the very latest!) by 31st January 2018.

When do I need to pay my tax?

You will need to pay your income tax by the filing deadline date. For example, for the period 6th April 2016 to 5th April 2017 you will need to pay tax due for this period by 31st January 2018.

When do I need to file my VAT return?

If you are VAT registered you will be required to file a VAT return every 3 months. If you have a VAT liability (i.e. the VAT you charge on your income is more than the VAT you reclaim on your costs) you will need to pay this 1 month and 7 days after the end of the reporting period. For example, for the three months 1st January to 31st March, you will need to make sure the return is filed and VAT paid by 7th May.

When do I need to file my company accounts?

Usually accounts are drawn up to cover a 12 month period, and you can decide which period end you want to prepare the accounts to. You have 9 months and 1 day to file your accounts with Companies House. For example, if your year end was 31st December 2016, you would need to make sure your accounts are filed by 1st October 2017.

When do I need to pay company tax?

A company is required to pay tax on its profits 12 months and 1 day after the end of its accounting period. For example, if your year end was 31st December 2016, you will need to have paid the tax by 1st January 2018.

Should I be using a limited company to reduce my tax?

It is true that there are opportunities to significantly reduce your total tax payable, but this is not always the case. There are occasions when using a UK company can actually increase the amount of tax payable—for example if you earn less than a certain amount of income, if you are going overseas, if you are holding assets for the long term, if you can't keep the profits in the company or if you want to make significant pension contributions.

What are my legal responsibilities as a company director?

As a director of a limited company, you are required by law to:

- Try to make the company a success, using your skills, experience and judgement
- Follow the company's rules, shown in its articles of association
- Make decisions for the benefit of the company, not yourself
- Tell other shareholders if you might personally benefit from a transaction the company makes
- Keep company records and report changes to companies house and HMRC
- Make sure the company's accounts are a 'true and fair view' of the business' finances
- Register for Self-Assessment and file a personal tax return each year

You can hire other people to manage some of the day-to-day things (e.g. an accountant) but you're still legally responsible for your company's records, accounts and performance.

What if I've lost my financial records?

If you can't replace your records you must do your best to provide figures. Tell HMRC when you file your tax return if you're using estimated figures (your best guess when you can't provide actual figures) or provisional figures (your temporary estimated figures while you wait for actual figures–you'll need to submit actual figures when available).

What is the difference between tax avoidance and tax evasion?

There is an important difference. Tax avoidance is the legitimate minimizing of your taxes using approved methods. Businesses avoid taxes by taking all legitimate deductions and by following the law.

Tax evasion, on the other hand, is the illegal practice of not paying taxes, by not reporting income and reporting expenses not legally allowed or by not paying taxes owed.

How much money will I earn through Spotify?

Spotify have a complicated model for paying royalties. They multiply their monthly revenue by your number of streams divided by the total streams on Spotify. Then, Spotify takes around 30% of this and pays the rest to your record company and publisher.

Spotify have published a pay-out range of between $0.006 to $0.0084 per stream for artists.

What can go wrong for me as a music artist in business?

Artists and musicians share the same concerns as any business owner.

What if I don't make any money and can't afford to pay my bills?

I am sure you are well aware that very few artists make enough money to support themselves, and fewer still make it big. If things start taking a turn for the worst, there are things you can do to remedy the situation. But first you should identify the source of the problem. Here are a few potential causes:

You're running out of money

Money keeps the wheels turning in your business and personal life, but yours may have ground to a halt. Consider how realistic you were with your income expectations. Also, it may be time to reassess your spending and cut costs where you can.

It is always scary to see numbers head into the red. But if you plan ahead, have a good head on your shoulders and listen to expert advisors, you can usually pull yourself out. It's the tough learning experience that will make you a better business person in the long run.

You didn't plan properly

Planning is essential, and if unexpected problems are coming up (or worse – the same problem keeps coming up over and over) this might be a sign that you need some expert help with your business planning.

The music has died

Perhaps things aren't what they used to be, and other commitments are tearing you away from your music. Maybe you feel that things aren't moving along as quick as you'd hoped and that you are treading water or even regressing. Or maybe the main reason for starting the band was to make a lot of money, and it isn't happening. These are all sure fire ways to lose motivation quickly.

Someone takes you to court

All creators of art will be ultra-protective about their creations and rights. Making sure you stay on the right side of the law can be a minefield. For example, there have been a number of recent court cases whereby artists have not had samples properly cleared before releasing their records. This has led to enormous litigation cases. This is where a good lawyer will earn his stripes. However, in the unfortunate event that you do get sued, having the right corporate entity could be enormously important.

If you have a limited company or limited liability partnership, the amount you are personally liable for depends on the value of your ownership in the company. To make it a little clearer, here is an example:

A company limited by shares issues 100 shares to you valued at £1 each and you pay £100 for these when you set up your company. If your company goes bust, the maximum amount *you* would have to pay towards any outstanding bills is £100. This is even the case if the value of these shares is perceived to be much more than £100.

Despite the various challenges facing you and the fact that sometimes things often won't work out as you'd hoped…life goes on. Many famous artists have suffered from massive financial missteps and mishaps. Success is not about avoiding failure, but more so about recovering from times of failure. But you can put yourself in the best position possible if you equip yourself with the right tools and provide yourself with a first rate defence by using the skills of your professional team, which can be of enormous comfort in times of uncertainty.

CONCLUSION

So we have now reached the end of the informational part of this short book. I hope that your eyes are now wide open to some of the issues and challenges facing you when establishing your music business.

To summarise, we have looked at whether you have a business, the implications of ignoring the fact that you have a business and what you need to do to move things along—this starts with getting your business structure right. I have highlighted to you some of the main business challenges you'll face as your career starts to take off and looked the types of income and costs you are likely to come across as an artist. We discussed the importance of your professional business team, the roles they play and, importantly, when you need to hire them. I've explained how financial information can be used to your advantage, the administration you need to keep a handle on and what you should be asking your professional business team for.

Ultimately, every artist has unique challenges at every stage of their career. To get the most out of this book keep it to hand as reference or perhaps re-read it every now and again. Over the next few pages I have defined some key business terms and provided some simple examples of some financial reports to help you further.

All that is left to say now is that I wish you the best of luck on your journey to becoming a superstar!

KEY BUSINESS TERMS

Accountant: a business advisor who helps you set up your business structure prepares your accounts, tax returns and any other business and financial matters.

Advance: this is a loan, normally from a record label or publisher to an artist, to be repaid (recouped) from record sales or publishing royalties in respect of publishing.

Balance Sheet: this is a financial statement that shows a snapshot of your business' financial position at any one point in time.

Break Even: the point at which income and costs are equal and there is neither a profit nor a loss.

Business Manager: this is usually the person who drives the work of others in your professional business team in order to run your business more efficiently.

Cash Flow: the total amount of money flowing in or out over a period of time.

Commission: a mutually agreed upon fee payable to your manager, business manager, agent or other sales person for their services, often based on the income they facilitate for you.

Companies House: is the UK's official government organisation that keeps a record of all UK companies and information about them, which is why any company that wishes to become a limited company must, by law, be registered with Companies House.

Copyright: music copyright gives creators and owners legal backing for certain restrictions on copying.

Corporation tax: the tax levied on a company's profits, currently 20% in the UK.

Financial Advisor: a qualified professional who can help you with your investment decisions.

Financial Projections / Forecasts: 'business speak' for looking at the future financial position of your business.

Financial Statements: a formal record of the financial activities of a business person, company or partnership, usually referring to the profit and loss account, balance sheet and statement of cash flow.

Financial Year End: a business can choose its financial year end, usually covering a 12 month period (it can be longer or shorter under certain circumstances), but traditionally they are aligned with the tax year, i.e. 31 March and the calendar year 31 December.

HMRC: Her Majesty's Revenue and Customs is the government department responsible for the collection of taxes.

Income tax: the tax levied directly on personal income, the highest rate of which is currently 45% in the UK.

Limited Company (Ltd.): a private company whose owners are legally responsible for its debts only to the extent of the amount of capital they invested.

Limited Liability: the condition when business owners are legally responsible for the debts of the business only to the extent of the amount they have invested in the business.

Limited Liability Partnership (LLP): a partnership in which some or all partners aren't personally liable for the debts the business can't pay – their liability is limited to the amount of money they invest in the business.

Loss: amount of money lost by a business.

Partnership: a type of business organization in which two or more individuals manage and operate the business with the aim of making a profit, and which, by law, all owners are equally liable for the debts of the business.

PAYE: the government system, as required by law, for holding back tax on income payments (such as wages) to an employee.

Performance Income: income earned from playing a live show or making a personal appearance.

Performing Rights Society: the organizations that provide the function of collecting royalties for copyright holders from parties who wish to use copyrighted works publicly.

Profit: the surplus made after deducting all your costs from your income.

Profit and loss report: a financial statement that summarises your income, costs and expenses over a period of time, usually a quarter or a year.

Professional Advisor: a person who gives advice in a particular field of expertise that they have usually had training in, such as lawyers, accountants, stock brokers and insurance agents.

Promoter: these individuals stage events.

Publisher: they invest in writers, promote songs and collect earnings from publishing copyrights.

Royalty: a payment made to the legal owner of property, such as a copyright in a musical composition.

Self-Assessment: the calculation of your own tax liability, which is required every year if you have your own business.

Sole trader / Sole proprietor: a person who is the exclusive owner of a business and is entitled to keep all profits after tax has been paid but is also liable for all losses.

Tax Advisor: a financial expert specially trained in tax law.

Tax Treaty: an agreement made between two countries to resolve issues involving double taxation, generally determining the amount of tax that a country can apply to a taxpayer's income and wealth.

Tax Year: not to be confused with business financial year, this is the time period covered by a particular tax return: e.g. in the UK the tax year is from 6th April to the following 5th April.

Trademark: protection for the misuse of a business name which could confuse potential customers.

Trading Status: this refers to whether you are in business or not. To consider whether you are trading or not, they ask the following: do you have a realistic intention to make profit, do you have repeated transactions, and are you trading goods that are clearly goods, are you comparable to other businesses in your activities?

VAT: Recoverable on the purchases you make, Value-Added Tax is the tax charged on goods and services, the standard VAT rate of which is 20% in the UK.

Withholding tax (WHT): tax deducted at the source by a country that you do not live in.

EXAMPLES OF FINANCIAL REPORTS

EXAMPLE OF A PROFIT & LOSS REPORT

	2016	
	£	£
TURNOVER		
Live income	75,750	
Recording income	20,000	
Publishing income	25,000	
Other income	2,753	
		123,503
COST OF SALES		
Live costs	26,700	
Recording costs	10,463	
Management commission	18,246	
Other commission	6,006	
		(61,415)
GROSS PROFIT		62,088
OVERHEADS		
Directors salaries	7,750	
Travel and subsistence	5,300	
Printing, stationery and postage	145	
Foreign tax credits	744	
Entertaining	514	
Accountancy fees	3,776	
Equipment repairs	275	
Legal and professional fees	875	
Bank charges	206	
Depreciation	2,000	
Foreign currency gains/losses	243	
		(21,828)
OPERATING PROFIT		40,260
Bank interest receivable		3
PROFIT BEFORE TAX		40,263
Taxation		(8,555)
PROFIT FOR THE PERIOD		31,708

EXAMPLE OF A BALANCE SHEET

	2016	
	£	£
FIXED ASSETS		
Tangible assets		**8,000**
CURRENT ASSETS		
Debtors	**17,533**	
Cash at bank	**23,084**	
	40,617	
CREDITORS: Amounts falling due within one year	**(16,809)**	
NET CURRENT ASSETS		**23,808**
TOTAL ASSETS LESS CURRENT LIABILITIES		**31,808**
CAPITAL AND RESERVES		
Called-up equity share capital		**100**
Profit and loss account		**31,708**
SHAREHOLDER'S FUNDS		**31,808**

EXAMPLE OF A CASH FLOW PROJECTION

	January £	February £	March £
Beginning cash balance	**4,750**	**11,705**	**14,172**
Receipts			
Live income – Minimum Guarantees	10,000	5,000	20,000
Merchandise sales	1,500	750	3,000
Tour support fees	-	-	5,692
Total cash in	**11,500**	**5,750**	**28,692**
Expenditure			
Management commission	1,725	863	3,450
Agency commission	1,000	500	2,000
Travel costs	800	900	1,250
Promotional costs	750	750	750
Accountancy fees	120	120	120
Legal fees	150	150	150
Corporation tax payment	-	-	29,890
Total cash out	**4,545**	**3,283**	**37,610**
Cash inflow/(outflow)	**6,955**	**2,467**	**(8,918)**
Closing cash balance	**11,705**	**14,172**	**5,254**

PELL**ARTISTS**

www.pellartists.com

info@pellartists.com

46339417R00059

Made in the USA
Charleston, SC
16 September 2015